Erratum

Page 3; Peter Flemming was educated at Eton College, not Eaton as stated.

Page 120; Stratford St. Andrew Patrol incorrectly states that Sgt Percy Kindred was Patrol Leader when in fact it was Sgt Herman Kindred.
Percy Kindred was the patrol's Corporal.

Churchill's Secret Auxiliary Units Including Special Duties Branch In Norfolk and Suffolk

Evelyn Simak & Adrian Pye

Published in 2013 by E Simak & A Pye

Printed by Lavenham Press Ltd

ISBN 978-0-9558797-7-7

Acknowledgements

This book would not have been written without the help of the Norfolk and Suffolk auxiliers – Harold Sewell, Hedley Smith, Arthur Wilson, D Fake, Mike Reeman, Claude Riches, Lennie Hall, Ted Pipe, Ron Watson, Charles Coe and Roy Double, Billy Hammond (SD Branch) and Jim Watson (Scout section) - who we had the honour of interviewing and we wish to thank them most profoundly for their time and patience. Our heartfelt thanks go to Jill Monk, John and Shirley Everett and Ivan Mower for their hospitality, and to all auxiliers' families, relatives and friends who kindly shared with us their treasured memories and memorabilia. We would also like to offer our grateful thanks to all the Norfolk and Suffolk farmers, landowners, gamekeepers and estate managers, and to English Heritage and National Trust for kindly permitting access onto their land. Sincere thanks are due to David Hunt for generously sharing his expert knowledge as a ret⸺ ⸺rld War 2 and Aux Units research. A ⸺ omen of the British Resistance Archive, ⸺ and in particular to Stephen Lewins an⸺ ⸺o the Trustees of the British Resistance ⸺ permitting access to their archive; and ⸺ ⸺al Archives and the Imperial War Muse⸺ ⸺ we have met in the course of our resea⸺ ⸺ation and advice. To list them all by nam⸺

We have taken cop⸺ ⸺s been made to trace copyright holders. ⸺ ⸺rtently, be less than adequate.

Some excerpts of p⸺ ⸺g's diary were taken from Adrian Hoare's book 'Standing up to Hitler' (for details see *Select Bibliography*) by kind permission of the author and his publishers, Countryside Books (Newbury, Berkshire).

The map used for the cover design is the OS new paper edition one-inch map of England and Wales – Norwich, Sheet 126 © Crown copyright 1945

Contents:

Preface

Much has been written in recent years about the Auxiliary Units set up by Prime Minister Winston Churchill during the time when the threat of Great Britain being invaded by Nazi Germany was imminent. As all these activities were secret and hence covered by the Official Secrets Act it has taken decades for more detailed information to surface, and yet, many questions will perhaps remain forever unanswered.

Auxiliary Units (AU) belonged to GHQ Home Forces. All AU members were meant to stay behind in the event of an invasion. Some were to sabotage and harass the enemy. Others were to spy on him using observers and secret wireless networks. They are referred to in contemporary documents as the Auxiliary Units (AU) operational patrols, the Special Duties Branch Auxiliary Units, the ATS Auxiliary Units and the Signals Section Auxiliary Units. *(Appendix A)*

The Auxiliary Units operational patrols consisted entirely of civilians working under the mantle of the Home Guard, the uniform of which they wore. Their Group leaders and Intelligence Officers were regular Army. Auxiliary Units Scout Sections comprised entirely of Army regulars assisted the operational patrols. Auxiliary Units operational patrols, assisted by Scout Sections, formed the clandestine stay-behind sabotage network.

The secret stay-behind spy network was formed by the Special Duties Branch which comprised more than 3000 civilian observers (spies), civilian wireless operators, army regulars drawn from the Royal Corps of Signals (Auxiliary Units Signals) and female wireless operators, mainly drawn from the Auxiliary Territorial Service (ATS), the women's branch of the army in WW2 - although some are believed to have come from the First Aid Nursing Yeomanry (FANY) and from the VAD (Voluntary Aid Detachments). Some others were civilian women who were not engaged in war work.

AU Signals were responsible for providing the communications to enable the civilian observers to pass their information to military HQs. For this purpose the Signals organisation was divided into areas that closely corresponded with existing Command areas. In each area there was a Signals officer in charge, with small headquarters of a sergeant, an instrument mechanic and a driver. Each area had a varying number of maintenance parties of three men each who were responsible for manning an IN-Station and for maintaining all OUT and SUB-OUT-Stations in their own areas.

On 29 August 1941, Field Marshal Lord Alanbrooke (then General Sir Alan Brooke) visited both units in his function as Commander in Chief of Home Forces, noting in his diary:

> "Left at 8.30am to spend a day with the auxiliary units in Kent and Sussex. These units comprise two main elements – one an information one equipped with wireless, and another a sabotage one equipped with explosive and weapons. Both are intended to work behind the enemy in the event of an invasion."

Thankfully, the invasion never happened and the Auxiliary Units remained untested.

How it all began

"The regular defences require supplementing with guerrilla type troops, who will allow themselves to be overrun and who thereafter will be responsible for hitting the enemy in the comparatively soft spots behind zones of concentrated attack." (*Winston Churchill to Anthony Eden, 25 September 1940*).

On 10 May 1940, Winston Churchill became Prime Minister of Great Britain. By 26 May the British Expeditionary Force (BEF) and the French First Army were bottled up in a corridor to the sea near the town of Dunkirk, about 60 miles deep and 15 to 25 miles wide. A decision was made by the War Office to evacuate the British troops, a mission that was completed on 4 June 1940. Huge supplies of equipment and ammunition had to be left behind and the army equipment available to the troops at home was only sufficient to equip two divisions.

After the evacuation from Dunkirk it became apparent to the War Office that Hitler might soon launch an invasion of Britain. Hitler's armies were only about 30 miles away across the English Channel and now they had the tactical benefit of being able to use French air bases to operate from. It was widely believed that an invasion would follow shortly, either in July or August. On the occasion of a lunch meeting between the Prime Minister and Lieutenant-General Andrew Thorne (Commander of XII Corps - part of Home Forces in the early years of World War II, with Lieutenant-General Bernard Montgomery as its commander), it transpired that Churchill was not confident that British troops could adequately defend all the English beaches.

Thoughts of creating a stay-behind resistance force were taken into serious consideration, taking inspiration from recent history such as the activities of Lieutenant Colonel Thomas Edward Lawrence (*better known as Lawrence of Arabia*), who during the Arab Revolt against Ottoman Turkish rule (1916–18) fought with Arab irregular troops in extended guerrilla operations. Another convincing example of the effectiveness of small units of an irregular force - which, although unable to beat the enemy, could nevertheless annoy him and force him to waste men and resources – comes from the Boer Wars where in 1900 and 1902 small commando units had with great success tied down more than a quarter of a million British and Dominion soldiers.

A document (dated 8 August 1940 and marked "SECRET"), which details some of the background leading to the formation of Auxiliary Units, has survived. It is a letter to the Prime Minister, written by Baron Duncan-Sandys, who was a minister in successive Conservative governments in the 1950s and 1960s, and for some years, the son-in-law of Winston Churchill. In 1937, Sandys was commissioned into the 51st (London) Anti-Aircraft Brigade, Royal Artillery, Territorial Army and during WW2 he fought with the British force in Norway, where he was wounded in action, giving him a permanent limp. His father-in-law gave him his first ministerial post during the wartime Coalition Government and he was also Chairman of a War Cabinet Committee for defence against German flying bombs and long-range rockets. Baron Duncan-Sandys lost his seat in the 1945 general election and resigned his commission as a Lieutenant Colonel in 1946.

The plans of creating stay-behind parties and the need to raise independent groups for action behind enemy lines resulted in the establishment of the Special Operations Executive (SOE), whose task it was to co-ordinate undercover operations in enemy territory. General Ironside (the Commander-in-Chief Home Forces, later Field Marshal William Edmund Ironside, 1st Baron Ironside GCB, CMG, DSO) also encouraged the development of small guerrilla forces - his version entailing the establishment of mobile columns, the so-called 'Ironside' units. However, lacking both the required equipment and the necessary support nothing ever came of this idea.

Finally, encouraged by Churchill, General Andrew Thorne and General Hastings Lionel "Pug" Ismay, the then Secretary of the Committee of Imperial Defence, discussed and consequently planned the setting up a covert resistance force, and finally a young officer believed to fit all requirements was chosen by Col Gubbins and given the task of creating a secret stay-behind army. The officer was Peter Fleming, who at the time was employed by Military Intelligence (Research), in short, MI(R) – a semi-secret branch within the War Office.

"Strix" - Capt Peter Fleming

Robert Peter Fleming was the brother of Ian Fleming, author of the James Bond novels. Educated at Eaton College and at Christ Church, Oxford, he was the editor of the "Eton College Chronicle" and later worked for "The Spectator" and as a special correspondent for "The Times, using his assumed penname "Strix". He also authored a series of books on his travels around the world as well as works of fiction and history. During WW2, Peter Fleming served with the Grenadier Guards before he was posted in, at the request of Col Colin Gubbins, to help establish the Auxiliary Units, and later served in Norway and Greece. His principle service, however, was as head of "D Division" when, from 1942 until the end of the war, he was in charge of military deception operations in Southeast Asia. He was awarded the Chinese military honorary Order of the Cloud and Banner, and an OBE for his services in 1945. Peter Fleming died in 1971 while on a shooting expedition near Glencoe in Argyll, Scotland.

Peter Fleming was considered by Col Gubbins to be the best candidate to assist with establishing a British guerrilla unit, in particular one comprising men who would be familiar with, and able to live off the land. Consequently, his first task was to find reliable men, to supply them with assorted explosives and incendiaries, to train them in the use of their new weapons, and to provide them with some sort of hidden base.

A secluded farmhouse in Bilting, Kent, served as Peter Fleming's first regional training centre. The house was called The Garth. Originally a cottage that was enlarged over time, the floorboards in the older wing had been removed - exposing joists, beams and roof-rafters - giving the rooms an exceptional height. All rooms were crammed full with explosives and weapons. Wooden crates full of explosives served as tables and chairs. There was no electricity and candles provided the only lighting available.

In his recollections, Capt "Mad" Mike Calvert DSO - a Royal Engineers officer and demolitions expert who was part of Peter Fleming's group at The Garth – recalls:

> "There was no country-house atmosphere about our headquarters. Our stand-ins for furniture were boxes of gelignite, which is perfectly safe as long as it is treated the right way. On one occasion we had a visit from several VIPs and decided we would have to do the right thing and offer them a meal and we all sat down round the box of gelignite that we were using as a table. Soon after we had started it began to get dark so I lit a few candles and put them on the box. This was normal practice for Peter and me and we went on eating without giving a second thought to the spluttering candle flames. Looking back I realise that our guests, not used to living on quite such intimate terms with high explosives, behaved very well in the circumstances. "I see you like to live dangerously" was the dry comment made between mouthfuls by General Sir Andrew Thorne, Commander of XII Corps (Kent and Sussex).

The first groups to be trained at The Garth were known by the cover name of "XII Corps Observation Units". The name eventually chosen for the secret resistance force was "Auxiliary Units". These units were to be entirely composed of civilians and their mission would be to attack invading forces from behind their own lines while conventional forces fell back to the last-ditch GHQ Line. Their list of targets included aircraft and airfields, fuel dumps, railway lines, bridges and depots as well as local country houses, which might be used by German officers. Each unit was to work as an autonomous and self-contained cell within a radius of about 5 miles (8 km) from their underground operational base.

It is in this context interesting to read a first-hand account written by Peter Fleming himself (in "Invasion 1940") of which the following is an excerpt:

"How long it would have been before the spirit of open resistance among the British population in occupied territory would have been broken and driven underground no one can say… Before the Second World War the British Army's experience of guerrilla warfare had been largely confined to playing, often on a note of exasperation but generally in the end with success, the Sheriff of Nottingham to a series of Robin Hoods in Asia and Africa… So the British, as in war the weaker side often does, devoted some thought to the possibilities of guerrilla warfare (which at higher levels of the General Staff was generally referred to as 'scallywagging'), and it was because a few minds in the War Office, as well as Churchill's outside it, were already working along these lines … The first officer to see that it might temporarily be very valuable, and would certainly be better than nothing, was General Andrew Thorne … and he accordingly made known to the War Office his requirement for an officer to organise among the natives of Kent and Sussex a network of 'stay-behind parties' whose object would be to harass the enemy's preparations for the second phase of his advance on London.

'Auxiliary Units', as they were noncommittally designated, were controlled and administered by a small staff under the aegis of GHQ Home Forces. In the very early days, when they were little more than a bright idea, they were envisaged as being immediately expendable … and the pioneers in the XII Corps area argued that so ephemeral an effort was hardly worth making. Invoking the aid of an imaginary Chinese general of the fifth century, to whom they attributed the maxim "A guerrilla without a base is no better than a desperate struggler", they submitted a case for the construction of underground hideouts, to be stocked with rations, blankets, cooking stoves and so on, as well as with explosives, sabotage equipment and wireless sets. Based on these subterranean retreats, they contended, the guerrillas would have a sporting chance, not merely of inflicting one suicidal pinprick but of remaining a thorn in the enemy's flesh for weeks or perhaps even in some cases for months. Higher authority had, for the best of reasons, never heard of the Chinese general but was unlikely, for reasons almost equally good, to admit this… As a theatre for guerrilla warfare the United Kingdom suffers from the fundamental disadvantage of being much too small… Even in the least promising areas, however, some possibilities existed for operating by stealth against the invaders before they had consolidated their grip on the country…

There were in all 20-odd Auxiliary Units. The basic organisation in the summer of 1940 was one officer, with what was grandiloquently known as a "striking force" of some 12 soldiers commanded by a subaltern; as wireless sets with the necessary range became available, two signallers were added. Loosely affiliated to this military nucleus, and dotted arbitrarily about its sphere of operations (which often covered a whole county) were small "cells" composed of members of the Home Guard, selected for their resourcefulness, their knowledge of the country and their skill in field craft…

The underground hideouts to which both the "striking force" and the far-flung "cells" would withdraw when the regular forces fell back covered, loosely, the coastal hinterland of the two counties. They were mostly sited in areas of dense woodland or scrub. They varied in design. Some were merely large dugouts, excavated, roofed and provided with bunks and ventilation by the Royal Engineers... The domestic economy of these lairs bore a general resemblance to that of the Lost Boys' subterranean home in the second act of Peter Pan...

It seems unlikely that in practice the Auxiliary Units would have been able to achieve very much. Their main operational handicap would have been the lack of communication ... As long as the leaf was on the trees - for six or seven weeks that is, after the first landings on 21 September - their hideouts might well have remained undiscovered ... but with the onset of winter low-flying reconnaissance aircraft, aided by improved intelligence, would sooner or later have located the well-defined tracks which by that time would have converged on every woodland lair and it would have been only a matter of time before the guerrillas were hunted down. Even more damaging - and more swiftly damaging - to their prospects would have been the policy of reprisals, from which as we have seen, the Germans had no thought of shirking... Nevertheless, even assuming that the British resistance movement would have melted away in the white heat of German ruthlessness, it might have struck some useful blows before doing so... It is difficult to find fault with Churchill's estimate of Auxiliary Units as "a useful addition to the regular forces".

Capt (later Lt-Colonel) Norman JL Field succeeded Peter Fleming as Officer Commanding XII Corps Observation Unit. It was Capt Field who had met General Alan Brooke on the occasion of his visit to Auxiliary Units in Kent *(see Preface):*

"I had decided to take him to meet a patrol of foresters at their base but just before his arrival a major appeared and advised that he had the authority to take charge for a while, would I follow? The major took the general into 'Hilltop' where they were met by two young ladies in FANY uniforms. The women were members of a parallel organisation (Special Duties Branch) to provide means of passing information from agents. Such was the security that we knew nothing about it." (Recording by Stephen Sutton 1995, Imperial War Museum).

Fleming's office at The Garth is described as having been a room containing two barrack tables. AU – believed to be the world's first resistance organisation ever to be established in advance of an invasion - were set up in great haste and secrecy, and with the help of much improvisation. Vehicles had to be requisitioned and explosives obtained. Everything had to be done in great hurry, and explosives and weapons were deposited in cellars and other obscure buildings in the area. The construction of an operational base would be undertaken only after suitable recruits to man it had been found. In his memoirs, Mike Calvert recalls that the Resistance Army of Kent and Sussex had at its core some of the toughest and most determined men he had ever met.

GHQ Auxiliary Units were one of altogether nine British secret services operating during WW2. The name was chosen because it was (deliberately) nondescript. AU members - civilians and servicemen and women alike – had to sign the Official Secrets Act, binding them to conditions of secrecy not only during the time of their service but for life. Under the premise that in order to function properly a secret service must remain secret forever, the plethora of information held in the Whitehall archives was intended to be kept there forever - including almost everything connected with AU. However, in all likelihood many files were destroyed at AU's disbandment.

"Gubsky" - Colonel Colin McVean Gubbins

The key figure in establishing a nation-wide resistance organisation was Col (later Major General) Sir Colin McVean Gubbins KCMG, DSO, MC, a SOE (Special Operations Executive) officer in the employ of MI(R).

Gubbins was born in Tokyo and educated at Cheltenham College and at the Royal Military Academy in Woolwich. Commissioned into the Royal Field Artillery in 1914 he served as a battery officer on the Western Front, where he was wounded and later awarded the Military Cross. In 1919, he joined the staff of General Sir Edmund Ironside in the North Russia Campaign. After a period spent at signals intelligence at GHQ India, Gubbins graduated from the Staff College at Quetta in 1928, and in 1931 was appointed GSO3 in the Russian section of the War Office. After his promotion to Brevet Major in 1935 he joined MI1, the policy making branch of the military training directorate. In October 1938, in the aftermath of the Munich Agreement, he was sent to the Sudetenland as a military member of the International Commission. After his promotion to Brevet Lieutenant-Colonel he joined G(R) — later to become MI(R) — in April 1939, where he prepared training manuals on irregular warfare including "The Partisan Leader's Handbook", "The Art of Guerrilla Warfare" and "How To Use High Explosives", the latter co-authored by Millis Jefferis *(Major-General Sir Millis Rowland Jefferis KBE, MC)*, an MI(R) explosives expert. Interestingly, all three booklets were translated into many different foreign languages but they were never published in England.

After the mobilisation of the British forces in 1939, Gubbins was appointed Chief of Staff to the military mission to Poland, and following his return to Britain in October 1939 he was sent to Paris as the head of a military mission to the Czech and Polish forces under French command, and a year later tasked with setting up the "Independent Companies" - forerunners of the Commandos. In November 1940, Gubbins became acting Brigadier. Seconded to the Special Operations Executive he was directed by General Headquarters Home Forces to create an underground army, the Auxiliary Units. The name was chosen because it was considered to be a nondescript term that would not arouse unwelcome attention. General Sir Edmund Ironside, Commander-in-Chief Home Forces, was to provide men, training and supplies, asking in return for weekly progress reports, copies of which would be forwarded to Prime Minister Winston Churchill. In December 1940 Col Gubbins was succeeded by Lt Col CR Major (later Brigadier), from 1 Eastern Command. Serving as executive head of Special Operations Executive from 1943 until SOE was shut down in 1946, Gubbins retired from the Army and became the managing director of a carpet and textile manufacturer. Spending his last years at his home on the Isle of Harris, he died at Stornoway on 11 February 1976.

Despite intelligence suggesting that the Germans might attempt to use airborne forces to supplement their main sea-borne assault, Gubbins believed that the entire length of British coastline was vulnerable, and he prepared to set up AU patrols within a coastal strip approximately 30 miles deep, starting in southern England. Kent was considered to be the likeliest area for an invasion to take place. The second most vulnerable region was believed to be East Anglia, where Capt Andrew Croft was invited to set up an organisation similar to the one already established by Peter Fleming in Kent. In Sussex, Capt John Gwynn, who owned extensive land around Lewes and Arundel, was asked to follow suit. By the end of August 1940, AU patrols were operating from Brechin on Scotland's east coast to Land's End in the south, and from north of the Bristol Channel as far as Pembroke Dock.

The role of the operational patrols was to disrupt communications, destroy fuel and ammunition dumps and to harass and inconvenience the enemy in any way possible, but not to damage the essential infrastructure of the county. Bridges, rail and road links, canals and waterways, telephone lines and other existing lines of communications were to be left intact and in working order, as the Army's advance to push out the invaders would be made so much easier if it did not have to contend with blown bridges and destroyed roads.

Initially, the units were controlled by 12 officers with specialist skills whose task it was not only to recruit and train but also to set up new AU patrols in their respective areas of operation. In the early days some of these so-called Intelligence Officers (IOs), like Peter Fleming, came from the ranks of MI(R).

(Photo sources unknown)

Col Colin McVean Gubbins   Lt-Col GHB Beyts   Major Peter Wilkinson

Colonel Gubbins, who left Auxiliary Units in November 1940, was assisted by Sir Peter Wilkinson from the War Office (his personal military assistant) and by Bill Beyts MC, formerly an Indian Army officer with the 6th Rajputana Rifles. With the establishment of the Auxiliary Units under the control of GHQ Home Forces, Peter Wilkinson was given the task to set up a national organisation that Colonel Gubbins was to manage. Peter Fleming was already established at The Garth in Kent.

Auxiliary Units Timeline

In spring 1940, General Sir Andrew Thorne (late Grenadier Guards) set up XII Observation Corps to defend Kent and Sussex from the threat of Nazi invasion. First commander of XII Observation Corps was Peter Fleming. Later on in the year, on 1 July 1940, to be precise, the UK resistance forces were officially formed. Colonel Gubbins named them "The Auxiliary Units", organising training and supplies under the guise of the LDV (later re-named "Home Guard"). Consequently, Capt GH 'Bill' Beyts (Gubbins' GSO2) appointed and allocated about a dozen officers to coastal areas extending from Caithness to Wales.

Coleshill House *(date and picture source unknown)*

In autumn 1940, General Headquarters Home Forces, Auxiliary Units (GHQ HF AU) moved from London to Coleshill House, a country estate with a large manor house near Swindon in Wiltshire. The house was owned by the Earl of Radnor, but only the Earl's two sisters and their dogs lived there. Col Gubbins chose Coleshill House because it was surrounded by extensive parklands and woods, making it very suitable for guerrilla training. In the early days, when an invasion was believed to be imminent, speed was of the essence, and the number of men who had to be trained necessitated that they meet at a central point. A great deal of mixing of one lot with another lot occurred, both at Coleshill and at The Garth. Secrecy was maintained wherever possible and new recruits did not report directly to Coleshill House but rather to the Post Office at nearby Highworth, where they reported to the postmistress, Mrs Mabel Stranks, who arranged for the unit transport that would take them to Coleshill.

PATROL LEADERS' COURSE

First Day

1930	Dinner	
2030	Opening Address	Commander or G.S.O.l.
	Lecture on Orders	G.S.O.l or G.S.O.2.Trg.
2130	Patrol Leaders prepare their orders.	

Second Day

0800	Breakfast	
0900	Elementary Drill	Capt. Lord Delamere
0945	Patrol Leaders give out their orders	(Major Oxenden (Capt. Lord Delamere
1100	Break	
1115	Lecture on Explosives	Capt. Kneale
1300	Lunch	
1400	Lecture on Daylight Reconnaissance and Camouflage	Major Oxenden
1500	Daylight Movement	Major Oxenden
1545	Practical Explosives	Capt. Kneale
1630	Tea	
1730	Weapon Training	Capt. Lord Delamere
1930	Dinner	
2030	Brains Trust, after which Patrol Leaders prepare Lecturettes	

Third Day

0800	Breakfast	
0900	Elementary Drill	Capt. Lord Delamere
0900	Lecturettes by Patrol Leaders	
1200	Snack Lunch	

Schedule of a Patrol Leaders' course held at Coleshill House (*note the high rank of the lecturers*).

SUBJECT:- Patrol exercise

TO:- All Operational I.Os.

The following system is being used by one I.O. with illuminating results, and the idea may be of interest and use to others.

The patrol is assembled - preferably in its O.B - and the I.O. arrives in the role of observer. His report on his day's observation, is something like this:-

" A goods train is being loaded with ammunition at 987321. About forty men are working on it.

The entrance to the railway tunnel at 456789 has been cleared, and trains, which had been held up, are moving again.

The racecourse is being used as a landing ground. Ten dive-bombers are already dispersed along the north side.

There is a rumour in the village that the whereabouts of our O.B. is known to some small boys; the father of one of them is held as a hostage, and his mother wants him to tell it to the enemy.

A high wireless mast, and an engine are installed on the hill at 234678.

The manor house at X is the H.Q. of a Div. corps or army commander.

That is all I ave to report. I am now going to bed. What do you propose to do about it?"

The patrol, under the P/L, are given about an hour to decide what they are going to attack, or whether they are going to move their home, or what they are going to do. The result of their conference may alter your opinion on their level of intelligence very considerably, one way or the other. Probably the other.

M. Oxenden

'Capt. G.S.

Headquarters.
27.5.42.

Document relating to a Patrol Exercise, issued by Capt Nigel Oxenden on 27 May 1942

The auxiliers commonly stayed at Coleshill for a long weekend to be trained in guerrilla-style warfare and in the use of weapons and explosives. Their teacher in unarmed combat was WE Fairbairn, the former commander of the Shanghai Police Riot Squads and an expert in every imaginable method of attack and defence. Fairbairn was co-inventor of the so-called Fairbairn-Sykes fighting knife which formed part of the equipment of all auxilers. Some of Fairbairn's teachings can be seen in his book "All-In Fighting" which is richly illustrated with line drawings. Besides unarmed combat the men were trained in the use of explosives and weapons. More than 100 Army officers and some 600 other ranks spent time on the premises, with some making repeated visits to the house. Throughout the relatively short life of the Auxiliary Units more than 5,000 recruits are believed to have been trained at Coleshill House. Sadly, the manorial house burnt to the ground soon after the war and only the stable block and outbuildings that once housed the administrative buildings survive.

John Everett from Alby Patrol (Norfolk Group 3) recalls his visits to Coleshill:

"I was fortunate to go to Coleshill repeatedly as other members of Alby Patrol were unable to do so. I visited Coleshill four or five times. On my first visit I was a Private in the Alby Patrol, and I was accompanied by members of other patrols within Group 3. We had RTO passes to travel and stayed at Coleshill from Thursday to Sunday.

We travelled by rail, reported to the Post Office in Highworth, and from there we were taken to our destination by military transport. On our arrival we were greeted by senior NCOs. Our accommodation was in Nissen huts in the grounds and our camp was guarded by Service personnel attached to Highworth House. We ate in the Officer's Mess which was situated in the main house. Our classrooms were in Highworth House *[sic]*.

There were commonly about 15 auxiliers on one course. Practical training was conducted in Nissen huts. There was a rifle and a grenade range and we also practised with revolvers. We marched to the ranges on foot. Explosives practice was also carried out in the grounds, and there were small tanks and other military vehicles, wrecked through use, where we were instructed to put our charges on.

In field craft and observation exercises, the enemy demonstrators were dressed in ex-German uniforms to make us familiar with our observations and we were also made familiar with German small arms.

We had an exercise to learn how to approach and destroy a target, which was carried out under the cover of darkness. The staff was very mixed and came from various regiments but mainly Infantry and Royal Engineers.

We used to have a daily parade, which I used to take when I became a Corporal. In front of Highworth House there was a big gravel square with a straight gravel drive leading to it, where the foot drill parade was held.

We most certainly gained a lot of experience in the way a patrol should operate. This information we would pass on to our fellow members in Group 3. But from a practical point of view a lot more was learned about explosives, weaponry and field craft from the permanent regular staff at the Norfolk HQ which was open to all members of Auxiliary Units. On reflection, in modern parlance it would probably be termed as a public relations exercise – hence dining in the Officers Mess! - that was not open to the public, not forgetting we had all signed the Official Secrets Act!"

By November 1940, 14 geographical areas had been created. With the exception of the inland regions north of the Bristol Channel *(Wales)*, each was assigned two Scout Sections, drawn from the County regiments and consisting of an officer and 11 other ranks, and transport.

Group Commanders were appointed and the first series of courses for Group Commanders were held at Coleshill in March 1941. In the second half of the year the 14 existing geographical areas covered by AU operational patrols were expanded to 22 areas, which, after a little reshuffling of Intelligence Officers (IOs) in the south-west they were reduced to 21 and finally to 20.

In the wake of "Operation Barbarossa" - the name given to Hitler's invasion of Russia on 22 June 1941 – the threat of invasion in Great Britain began to recede and when Colonel Lord Glanusk DSO took over from Lt Colonel CR Major in February 1942 it became obvious that the auxiliers had been, in some respects at least, overrated, leading to some confusion and inefficiency in action. For instance, tests revealed that after two years of

11

training, less appeared to be known about the use of explosives than in 1940 and that some of the 'toys' that had been issued would never, and could never successfully be used. Whereas auxiliers were once asked to devise 'booby traps' under the noses of enemy sentries their task was now to get in and place a unit charge. The Home Guard was warned to expect local raids, and all units worked out their raid roles whilst at the same time sceptics wondered if it would ever amount to anything more. However, IOs were still able to order and obtain all stores they wished for and to ask for any recruit from the ranks of the Home Guard they wanted for making up their numbers. The War Office had agreed to increase the number of patrols to extend into as yet uncovered areas such as the Borders, Northumberland and Durham. Some other regions had even become too large for one IO to deal and they were consequently divided up between two.

In July 1942 the Auxiliary Units operational patrols received their own training manual which was titled "The Countryman's Diary 1939". The cover cleverly disguised it as an agricultural supplies diary, published by "Highworth's Fertilisers". The diary's pages depict numerous examples of sabotage and demolition devices as well as ambush booby traps used by SOE agents in occupied Europe, various types of fuses, tube-igniters and detonators, plastic explosives and time pencils. One chapter was devoted entirely to calculating the precise amount of gelignite required for destroying a particular target.

With the steadily increasing number of AU operational patrols, more Group Commanders (GCOs) were required and many of the patrol leaders, who had previously shown that they were outstanding and capable men, were appointed to be Group Commanders. Their task was to maintain contact with all their patrols, and to use their extended command for organising attacks with the group's combined strength. Sometimes the local AU Scout Section was also involved. On average, every GCO was in charge of four to five patrols. When the leader left his patrol to become a GCO, a new patrol leader was appointed from the ranks of the remaining members to take his place and given the rank of Sergeant.

As the year progressed and the country's defences became stronger, the soldiers who had helped with local training were withdrawn, and the auxiliers now had to travel all the way to Coleshill House for more specialised training. As this was not always possible the IOs resorted to organising competitions between individual patrols. By now AU operational patrols were well-organised and self contained and prepared and able to fight alone and on their own. With the threat of invasion no longer imminent, IOs were directed to pay more attention to their men's turnout and advised to introduce drill practice. This was not very well received by the auxiliers.

By 1943, both the Norfolk and Suffolk operational patrols had been absorbed into GHQ Home Forces 202 Battalion, which covered an area extending from Northumberland to the Thames-Severn line. Because the auxiliers were extensively trained in sabotage techniques and in living off the land, their call-up for full-time regular Army service had at first been deferred. But by the time Lord Glanusk was succeeded by Colonel FWR Douglas, his GSO1 *(General Staff Officer Grade 1)*, in March 1943, a number of auxiliers had been called up and GCOs in many parts of the country were advised that the members of their patrols should be asked to volunteer for Special Forces service such as the Jedburgh teams, the SOE *(Special Operations Executive)*, the SAS *(Special Air Service)* or the Commandos. In some regions almost all of the auxiliers volunteered (and many lost their lives in action). Other patrols were disbanded and the members returned to the ranks of their local Home Guard.

By 1944, the prospect of an invasion had become unlikely, and on 12 July 1944 Commander Colonel Douglas announced at a special conference that the War Office had insisted on withdrawing most of the regular personnel currently with AU so as to meet the demands of the Army before D-Day. Plans were made to divide the formerly 20 regions along the coast into four regions only and so, during the last remaining months of their existence, Auxiliary Units were again organised by area instead of on a County basis, with Framlingham in Suffolk being the headquarters for East Anglia. Stores were provided for the following six months, and certain selected GCOs from each area were put directly under their TAA *(Territorial Army Association)* which ran the Home Guard. Norfolk's TAA was based at 22 Tombland in Norwich.

Soon thereafter the Auxiliary Units were stood down. On 18 November 1944, General Sir Harold Franklyn, Commander in Chief Home Forces, penned a letter to Colonel Douglas, which was circulated about a week later to every AU patrol member. It was accompanied by a letter from Colonel Douglas *(see page 152)*. Weapons and explosives were returned to headquarters, and many operational bases (OBs) were destroyed.

In April 1945, when the war in Europe was drawing to a close, the War Office, for the first time, announced to the press that a resistance force had existed in Britain since 1940. One of the first articles on the subject appeared in the "War Illustrated". It was titled "Now It Can Be Told!"

Little public interest appears to have been generated by these articles at the time and although snippets of inside stories gradually appeared in the media, it took 23 more years before the American author, David Lampe, who had already published on other WW2 subjects, including the Danish resistance organisation, wrote the first book on the subject. Lampe, like other authors later following in his footsteps, found that a number of auxiliers still regarded themselves as bound by the vow of silence and either purportedly knew nothing about a secret resistance organisation or bluntly refused to talk about their activities. The Official Secrets Act is still in force but information on AU was declassified in 1996.

Now it can be told

Contrary to popular belief, not all AU operational patrol members originated from the ranks of the Home Guard. They were, however, uniformed for cover as "Home Guard", and later absorbed into one of three "GHQ Special Reserve Battalions", with the distinctive numbers of 201 (Scotland and the North), 202 (The Midlands) and 203 (Southern Counties) worn under the county flash from spring 1943 onwards.

Before being approached, likely candidates were vetted by plain clothes or Special Branch police officers. The recruits were to be part-time volunteers, varying in age and occupation, with the main criteria being that they were fit and capable of coping with the harsh conditions anticipated. They were told that they were being selected for special Home Guard duties. This, however, was merely a cover. Auxiliers were never officially registered as Home Guard members, and because they were not enrolled as fighting men they were not strictly covered (and protected) by the Geneva Convention.

As part of their Home Guard cover, the men wore the standard 1940 pattern battle-dress blouse and trousers, with the FS side cap. They had standard black ammunition boots and either black or khaki-coloured leather gaiters. As a concession to the conditions under which they were intended to operate, either in training or, more commonly, in the construction of their underground hideouts, they were given battledress denims - denim overalls, comprising a separate blouse and trousers, worn over, in order to protect either their uniform or civilian clothing. The auxiliers also received black rubber short lace up boots with a waterproof tongue, ideal for construction work or for moving soundlessly over paved surfaces. The rubberised brown groundsheet/cape was also issued and some units wore a woollen cap-comforter with their denims.

Auxiliers carried no equipment other than webbing or a leather waist belt, supporting a leather pistol holder or a revolver holster. Insignia was minimal, with the cap badge being the standard badge of the county regiment, as was the custom for Home Guard units. Until October 1942, auxiliers wore only Home Guard shoulder titles and stripes for sergeants. They were not allowed to wear the county's distinguishing letters or the battalion numerals of local Home Guard units.

From spring 1943 onwards, however, patrol members were issued shoulder badges bearing the numbers of one of the three newly created AU.

> "'202' shoulder flashes will be worn below the 'N.K'. The explanation of this is that you are all Norfolk Home Guard. The '202' does not refer to a HG Battalion but refers to your position as regards GHQ Reserve Troops." (Lt AGD Greenshields, GCO Norfolk Group 4 on 26 March 1943).

Farmers, gamekeepers as well as poachers, school teachers, engineers, veterinarians, office workers and the occasional vicar or milk delivery man, in general, people who knew their local area intimately, were frequently chosen as the men who were intended to stay behind in the event of an invasion. Considering their local knowledge, farm workers and gamekeepers as well as poachers, of course, were well equipped to negotiate their operational area in total darkness. The region's IO would commonly recruit the man intended to be patrol leader. The patrol leader in turn would then find five or six suitable local men that he already knew well and trusted. Occasionally a farmer was leader of a patrol composed mainly of his own farm workers, and it is not unusual to find father and son, brothers or cousins within the same patrol.

AU operational patrols comprised between four and eight (rarely more) members. Once accepted, the men were asked to sign the Official Secrets Act. They were told that in case of an invasion they would be on their own, and most likely killed by enemy troops within a couple of weeks. The auxiliers trained locally, mainly at night time, and at Coleshill House, The Garth or at a more local training establishment at weekends.

Recruitment, training and exercises

John Everett's recollections of how he was recruited into his local AU operational patrol are perhaps representative for the majority of auxiliers:

> "I joined the LDV – Local Defence Volunteers, forerunner of the Home Guard – just before my 17th birthday. Our headquarters were in Alby church hall and our observation post on Alby church tower. Commander for the local area was Major Gurney of Northrepps Hall, a WW1 veteran who was later replaced by Major Ketton-Cremer of Felbrigg Hall. The lieutenant who had jurisdiction over Aldborough, Thurgarton, Alby/Thwaite and Hanworth was Mr Burrell Hammond, also a veteran of WW1. The members of Alby/Thwaite LDV were initially armed only with pickaxe handles and privately owned shotguns.
>
> Later we got rifles and I soon turned out to be an above average shot. By September 1941 I had been promoted to lance corporal. Around that time I was approached by a local farmer, Alec Scott about joining Auxiliary Units. I had, of course, known Mr Scott but had no idea that he was in AU.

The signing on 'ceremony' consisted only of signing the Official Secrets Act, by the roadside near the OB. This was witnessed by Capt Duncan (Group leader) and Alec Scott (patrol leader). As it turned out, I already knew four patrol members but had not known they were in Auxiliary Units".

The basic aim of Auxiliary Units' training was outlined in one of the three booklets authored by Colonel Gubbins for G(R) — later to become MI(R) — in April 1939. It is titled 'The Art of Guerrilla Warfare'.

The aim of the guerrilla must be to develop their inherent advantages so as to nullify those of the enemy. The principles of this type of warfare are therefore:

(a) Surprise first and foremost, by finding out the enemy's plans and concealing your own intentions and movements.

(b) Never undertake an operation unless certain of success owing to careful planning and good information. Break off the action when it becomes too risky to continue.

(c) Ensure that a secure line of retreat is always available.

(d) Choose areas and localities for action where your mobility will be superior to that of the enemy, owing to better knowledge of the country, lighter equipment, etc.

(e) Confine all movements as much as possible to the hours of darkness.

(f) Never engage in a pitched battle unless in overwhelming strength and thus sure of success.

(g) Avoid being pinned down in a battle by the enemy's superior forces or armament; break off the action before such a situation can develop.

(h) Retain the initiative at all costs by redoubling activities when the enemy commences counter-measures.

(i) When the time for action comes, act with the greatest boldness and audacity.

The partisan's motto is "Valiant but Vigilant"

Training was initially provided locally by the IOs of Auxiliary Units patrols, by regular Army troops and/or by members of the AU Scout Sections. The immediate training given by an IO was instruction in the use of the items contained in the cardboard boxes assigned to each unit, called "Aux Units Mark 1" and referred to as "packs". The first packs contained 10 lbs of Plastic Explosive and a variety of incendiary devices, as well as a hollow bronze casting resembling a lump of coal that could hold about two ounces of High Explosive and a detonator. A much-improved pack, referred to as "Aux Units Mark 2", was issued from summer 1941 onwards.

During the week the auxiliers trained at rifle ranges, in woods and disused gravel pits closer to home, usually at night. Patrols in Norwich Group often trained at the sand pits in Whitlingham Lane, which have since been transformed into Whitlingham Broad, a nature reserve and favourite area for walkers. Exercises were also held at various other locations, such as Roughton Heath. Little of Roughton Heath remains today because much of it was ploughed up during the war for food production. More than a dozen exercises were held on Plumstead Heath, which during the day was a shooting range.

Many Suffolk patrols trained at Aldeburgh, at Dunwich Heath or on nearby beaches. Disused gravel or clay pits on the outskirts of Eye were used for explosives training not only by Suffolk auxiliers but also by some Essex patrols (*AE Cocks, Churchill's Secret Army*).

John Everett recalls:

> "Basic training with explosives was done within the patrol, with more advanced training at the Norfolk headquarters. The practical training in the use of explosives was at Cawston Heath, although this was a limited form of training as the explosive charges used were only small. This training at both the headquarters and Cawston Heath would be undertaken at weekends, particularly Sundays, as it must be appreciated that patrol members were in full-time employment. For secrecy, the training of the various patrols at Cawston Heath was held with no other Home Guard or regular units being trained at the same time. The only others being on the heath at these times were the trainers."

On weekends, patrols regularly attended specialist training courses and summer camps at regional training centres such as Leicester Square Farm near the village of North Creake in north-west Norfolk, or at the rifle ranges on Cawston Heath (in Broadland district), at Weybourne or West Runton or at a small range located near the brick kiln at Blickling. All instructors were regular Army specialists, one of them being George Maskell, a Norwich man who had a black belt in judo.

Cawston Heath is an area of wood and heathland that features in many guidebooks and directories as the place where the last duel fought in Norfolk took place on 20th August 1698. The contestants were Sir Henry Hobart MP of Blickling Hall and Oliver Le Neve, a lawyer from Great Witchingham. In the 20th century the area was used as a military training ground. The Army had a firing range there but had to move out because the bullets were going over the top of the butts and landing on people and houses in the nearby village of Marsham. In the 1940s the heath was used for general training purposes and sometimes in joint exercises as well as for rifle practice by Army, Home Guard and AU operational patrols from both Norfolk and Suffolk. The earthen mound where soldiers fired at numbered targets can still be seen – the target was held up by a courageous volunteer sitting in the trench behind the mound. In 1986 Cawston Heath was designated as a Site of Special Scientific Interest. It is open to the public and traversed by many footpaths.

Various regular Army units were chosen as the "enemy", who, for the patrols in Norfolk Group 3, at least, was more often than not based at the nearby Wolterton Hall. During one such exercise the men from Alby patrol had to sneak up on three or four vehicles of the 1st Royal Army Service Corps, based at North Walsham, and to put chalk marks on them without being detected. Two patrol members were sent to mark the cars whilst the others were on lookout. J Everett recalls:

> "Other "enemies" included the Duke of Wellington's Regiment, the Manitoba Rangers (part of the Canadian Army) and the Household Cavalry (a unit that used armoured scout cars) and the Reconnaissance Corps."

A large exercise involving several patrols and about 50 men was held at Sculthorpe aerodrome before its completion in May 1943. The different participating patrols all used different map references for locating their individual set targets. During the day the men would, of course, do their everyday jobs at work or on the farm. Asked about what he'd been doing during the war, Herman Kindred (leader of Stratford St Andrew patrol, Framlingham Group, Suffolk) says:

"I was busy, very very busy. When we had an exercise on Sunday morning I was sometimes extremely tired. I looked after the horses on our farm and I had to get up early in the morning to feed them."

Herman Kindred also remembers one of his patrol's night exercises:

"We had a night exercise at Parham Hall one day. The depot was at Glemham Hall and all the officers slept at Parham Hall at the time, and they wished to test their security at night. We agreed on, I think, a 10 o'clock start. Two of our chaps knew the caretaker who opened the door for them and let them inside, and they got right in and left their notes on the sentries' table without being seen or caught. The officers were furious."

From the very start it was realised that the activities of AU operational patrols were dependent on finding suitable targets but Capt Oxenden thought it was perhaps too optimistic to expect that one man, who would be watching from a well-hidden observation post, would be successful in finding something worth attacking every day, day-in, day-out. Nevertheless, all exercises began with the assumption that a target had been found until, after two years, doubts were finally thrown upon the probability of one single static observer providing adequate to a task considered most important. During 1940, IOs were urged to experiment with messenger dogs, carrier pigeons, light signals, call-boxes and dead letter drops and even relay teams mounted on horses as the passing of information was considered to be of greater importance than the problem of obtaining it. This practice was soon to be abandoned.

Beeston Hall near Neatishead – one of the Norfolk Auxiliary Units HQs – in 2012.

Beeston Hall is a fine country mansion, accessed by a long private driveway and surrounded by pastures, woods and parkland. John Fielding of Earlham Patrol, Norfolk Group 1, Norwich, and other auxiliers remember it fondly and recall that the door was always open to them.

The rifle range on Cawston Heath (North Norfolk)

Auxiliary Units HQs and the location of many exercises. The farm buildings have since been converted into private dwellings. The picture, taken in 2012, shows one of the converted barns.

These men must have revolvers

Whole patrols as well as individual auxiliers were instructed in the use of weapons and explosives, in sabotage, how to set booby-traps, and in unarmed combat. Other training included methods of stalking and reconnoitring, camouflage, map reading and OB security. The main purpose for Auxiliary Units HQ, however, was to instruct the auxiliers in guerrilla warfare, and there is ample evidence that Major William Ewart "Dan" Fairbairn, the founder and former commander of the Shanghai Police Riot Squads, was in charge. Major Fairbairn had developed his own fighting system (known as "Defendu"), as well as other weapons; tactics including innovative pistol shooting techniques and, in cooperation with Eric A Sykes, he had designed the Fairbairn-Sykes Fighting Knife. Knife fighting and silent killing was reportedly under the command of Capt (later Major) WW "Bill" Harston, assisted by a sergeant major from Scotland who is said to have been specially released for the purpose from Barlinnie Prison in Glasgow. How well the patrols had absorbed their training was thoroughly tested at the end of each course.

Initially, many auxiliers, particularly those operating in rural areas, used their own weapons, including shotguns. They were supplied solid-shot cartridges (to complement the usual "buckshot" rounds). AU operational patrols had, however, always been given high priority in the provision of weapons and explosive devices, almost as soon as they were created. They were the first to be issued Sten guns, which replaced the Thompson submachine gun. Referring to a pamphlet concerning Sten guns, issued by the Army, Lt AGD Greenshields (GCO Norfolk Group 4) remarks: "This only praises the weapon and deals with no adjustment of faults, and I therefore consider it useless to issue it." They also got the "Sticky bomb" and phosphorous hand-grenades before anyone else did. All auxiliers were equipped with Fairbairn-Sykes fighting knives and many had homemade garrottes, fashioned from a two-foot length of thin piano wire, with a piece of a broomstick handle at each end for better grip.

By 1941 each patrol was to have received one American M1918 Browning Automatic Rifle, one Thompson submachine gun and two M1917 Enfield rifles. Not every unit, however, received the full complement of weapons issued. The list of small arms allocated to each patrol grew over time, and in 1941, during Lt Colonel (later Brigadier) CR Major's command, each fully manned patrol was expected to have

  7 x .38in revolvers (American)
  2 x .30in rifles (American)
  7 x fighting knives
  3 x knobkerries
  48 x No. 36 grenades (four-second fuses)
  3 x cases of S.T. grenades ("Sticky Bombs")
  2 x cases of A.W. bottles (Phosphorous grenades)
  1 x .22in rifle (silenced) from various manufacturers
  1 x .45in Thompson SMG (American)
  40 x .38in pistol rounds
  200 x .30in rifle rounds
  1,000 x .45in ACP rounds for the Thompson
  200 x .22in rounds

On noticing that Churchill had pencilled *"these men must have revolvers!"* in the margin of one of the weekly reports received from Colonel Gubbins, all auxiliers were subsequently issued with handguns, including 400 Colt .32in semi-automatics. Weapons deals made in various countries resulted in a large number of different makes and marks becoming available to Auxiliary Units' inventories. AU also appear to have received privately donated American weapons from the "Committee for American Aid for the Defense of British Homes", channelled through Section XII, one of SOE's secret stations at Acton House near Stevenage in Hertfordshire.

"Aux Units Mark 1" - the portable explosives kit

Explosives and incendiaries were to be the main offensive weapons used by the AU, whose primary role, after all, was to attack the enemy's stores, transport and communications. From mid-July 1940 onwards there was a plentiful supply of explosives and accessories and operational bases (OBs) or ammunition stores were crammed full with wooden boxes of explosives, incendiaries, fuses and detonators, pressure, pull and trip switches and trip wire. As has already been mentioned *(see page 15)*, every patrol was issued with the so-called "Aux Units Mk 1", later simply referred to as "packs". These packs consisted of an assortment of explosives and incendiary devices, fuses and detonators contained in cardboard boxes which soon disintegrated when buried or left out in the rain. Improved packs, called "Aux Units Mark 2" were issued in the summer of 1941, now contained in tin boxes and with their contents greatly revised. Each pack, basically a portable explosives kit, consisted of the following:

> 24 Copper tube igniters
> 1 Crimping tool
> 6 Striker boards
> 1 Tube Vaseline
> 1 Spool trip wire .032"
> 1 Spool trap wire .014"
> 8 Coils tape
> 12 Pocket time incendiaries
> 20 1-hr lead delays
> 50 3-hr lead delays
> 50' Instantaneous fuse (Orange Line)
> 240 ft Cordtex
> 100 Detonators (nos. 8 or 27)
> 20 lbs Explosive (Nobel 808, Polar Gelignite or Plastic)
> 1 Sandbag
> 6 Pull Switches
> 3 Pressure Switches
> 48 ft Safety fuze Mk II Bickford
> 20 C.E. Primers (two tins of 10 each)
> 24 Tubes, fuze, sealing, in Aux Units where the fuse is not packed in tins.

Approximate numbers of these packs for disposal at stand-down were estimated to be 630 in Norfolk and 510 in Suffolk.

The "Sticky Bomb" (designed by Major Millis Jeffries) was a six to eight inch diameter phosphorous filled glass ball covered with a thin metal sheet outer skin. Between the metal skin and the glass ball was a sticky material called birdlime. Projecting off the "bomb" was a handle with a firing lever that activated a time pencil. The idea of the "sticky bomb" was to remove the metal casing and then run up to a vehicle and hit the vehicle with the "bomb". The birdlime would adhere the "bomb" to the vehicle. Simultaneously, the lever would be operated and so activating the time fuse within a short time to allow the "bomber" to run off. An order for one million sticky bombs was placed in June 1940, but various problems delayed their distribution in large numbers until early 1941, and it is believed that fewer than 250,000 were ever produced. The "sticky bomb" proved dangerous to use and was later withdrawn. No 74 Grenade was another term used for the above-mentioned "sticky bomb". It contained Nobel's explosive with a minimal charge of phosphorous.

Gelignite was stored in the operational base (or in the ammo store if the patrol had one) along with other explosives, packed in wooden cases, with each cylindrical charge being wrapped in thick waxed brown paper. Some patrols also received nitro glycerine in stick form. It is also known as blasting gelatine or jelly. Invented by Alfred Nobel, the inventor of dynamite, in 1875, it was the first plastic explosive in a range of many more variations to follow. Gelignite consists of a type of gun cotton, dissolved in either nitro-glycerine or nitro glycol and mixed with wood pulp and sodium nitrate or potassium nitrate. Gelignite is easily mouldable and safe to handle without any protection and it is also one of the cheapest explosives available. It cannot explode without a detonator and is hence safe to store almost anywhere without having to take a number of safety precautions. Gelignite is commonly used in quarries and mines and it has for a long time been a favoured by revolutionaries and guerrillas.

One of the simplest plastic explosives was Nobel's Explosive No. 808, also known as Nobel 808. It was developed by the British company Nobel Chemicals Ltd well before World War II. Nobel 808 has a distinctive smell of almonds and looks like green plasticine. During World War II the British SOE extensively used it for sabotage missions. Captured SOE-supplied Nobel 808 is believed to have been the explosive used in the failed assassination attempt on Adolf Hitler in 1944.

Plastic explosive also referred to as putty explosive. It too resembled plasticine, being a soft and easily mouldable solid material that is particularly suited for demolition work. Engineers and combat engineers commonly use it for the demolition of obstacles and fortifications. In more recent times some terrorist groups are also known to have used plastic explosives. On average each Auxiliary Units patrol would be holding up to half a ton of various explosives in their OB or ammunition store. Plastic explosive remained secret for 15 years after the war.

RDX (Research Department Explosive) was used widely during WW2 as a priming explosive to boost the effect of another, often combined with TNT, and is one of the first plastic explosives.

Patrols were also issued with gun cotton and primers. Gun cotton is a slab-shaped explosive about the size of a book with a tapered hole in one flat side. A primer would be pressed into the tapered hole, followed by a detonator, and the fuse wire would be attached to the detonator. There were two versions: wet gun cotton and dry gun cotton. Gun cotton was intended to be used for blowing up railway lines.

Every auxilier was trained in the basic principles of making and using explosive and incendiary devices. They were issued with tins full of detonators (small aluminium tubes containing fulminated mercury) and the hand crimping tools to fit them to fuse wire and copper igniter primers. Some AU operational patrols also had Pot magnesium at their disposal - a paint can sized (approx 6" in diameter) incendiary device with an aperture to accept a detonator, the fuse being attached to the detonator being lit by hand. These were withdrawn as being too dangerous to use. Many explosive training courses were held at Coleshill House. Besides explosives, the AU patrols were also issued with various types of hand grenade.

No 36 Grenade, also known as the Mills Bomb, was a classic design. It looked like a cast iron pineapple with deep grooves, making it easier to grip. It had a central striker, held by a close hand lever and secured with a pin. A competent thrower could manage 15 metres (49 feet) with reasonable accuracy, but the grenade was known to throw lethal fragments farther than this. After throwing, cover had to be sought immediately. The grenade had a 4-second fuze for throwing and a 7-second fuze for firing from the rifle cup discharger.

The bodies of No 69 stun grenades were made from Bakelite. They were issued later during the war.

No 76 Grenade is also referred to as Self-igniting Phosphorous (SIP) Grenade. It was also known as Allbright-Wilson (AW) bomb. Basically, these were glass bottles containing a highly inflammable liquid composed of phosphorus, benzene, water and crude rubber lump. SIP had no fuze as the phosphorous ignited the benzene (a chemical derived from coal and petroleum, found in petrol and other fuels. Considered to be too dangerous for storage within the OB they were usually kept in the ammo store or within a metal container that was buried several hundred yards distant from the OB. More than six million grenades of this type were manufactured.

No 77 Smoke Grenade was issued to the Army as well as to the Home Guard. It was fitted with an "all-ways" percussion fuse, designed to set the grenade off when it hit the ground. The fuse was called "all-ways" because it set off the grenade no matter which way up it was when hitting the ground. It produced thick white smoke for about 30 seconds. Essentially, the grenade consisted of a tin with a screw-down lid, containing white phosphorous and a detonator. Smoke grenades were generally kept separate from other explosives.

Auxiliers also had a variety of Pull, Pressure, Release, Anti Personnel and Delay switches and time pencils at their disposal, as well as a number of wires, lines and cord required to initiate the function of a made-up charge or device.

Pull switches could be attached to trip wires and the charge was set off when a pin on the switch was pulled. Pressure switches were commonly placed underneath an object. When sufficient weight was put on top, the metal pin attached to the spring-operated striker was sheared and this in turn triggered the explosives connected with it. Release switches operated in reverse to the Pressure switches in that removing pressure from them triggered the explosive charge. Pressure switches were frequently used for making booby-traps.

As the name implies, Time Delay switches operated on the principle that a lead wire would stretch and break within a certain time and at a certain temperature. It is possible to quite accurately calculate the wire's breaking point. When the wire broke, a spring-retained striker pin would activate the charge. Time Delay pencils were supplied with a tag adhering to each one, stating the number of hours' delay before they would detonate.

Time pencils were metal tubes, about 6 inch long and with the diameter of an ordinary pencil. The time pencil consisted of a glass phial containing acid, which was connected to the body of the pencil. Beneath the phial there was a wire attached to an energised coil spring bearing onto a plunger. Fuse wire was crimped into the base of the metal tube, and the other end of the fuse was attached to a detonator, which in turn was placed into the explosive charge. Additionally, the metal tube had a sight aperture and a safety pin. To activate the process, the safety pin would be removed. This would break the glass phial, the acid would eat through the wire and release the spring that in turn would trigger the plunger. This would fire the fuse wire, which in turn would fire the detonator and lastly the explosive charge. The time pencils were coloured to denote the various timings they would take once the acid was released, typically 30 minutes to 11 hours. Under extremely cold conditions they would, however, take longer to operate whereas they would be considerably quicker in extreme heat.

The so-called Universal Switch was a device that combined the trigger variations of Pressure, Pull or Release switches. There was also a Fog Signal Switch which, when attached to orange line fuse, was used for demolitions carried out on railway lines. It was activated by the train running over the top of the rail-mounted switch.

Fuses are required in order to initiate the function of a made up charge or device. They consist of some kind of inflammable material, and depending on their chemical design some will work even when submerged in water. One of the commonest fuses is known as the Safety or Bickford Fuse, named after its inventor William Bickford from Tuckingmill, Cornwall.

Bickford fuse was made by civilian manufacturers, who in turn supplied the military as well as the mining industry. The fuse came in a slow and a fast burning version and the amount of time it took for the fuse wire to burn down was measured in seconds per feet. It had a black powder core and its coating, in contrast to other military fuses which are highly coloured and known as cords, was usually black or orange. The fuse burns at a speed of 60 to 90 seconds per foot. John Everett has noted in his memoirs that Bickford fuse was coloured black, Instantaneous fuse was coloured orange and Plastic fuse was silver-coloured.

Compared with the Safety fuse, detonating cord – also known as Cordtex and Primacord - burns at high speed and is used to detonate certain types of explosive without the use of a separate detonator. Because of its extremely high speeds it causes an almost instantaneous detonation after being activated. Fuse wire was always cut to length with a spark proof cutter, the cut being at 45 degrees across the wire.

Weapons and sabotage equipment intended for AU use was collected and packed at Acton House (SOE Section XII near Stevenage) and moved to AU HQs at Coleshill from where it was distributed to area IOs, who in turn supplied their patrol leaders.

Magnets, pull switch and fuse container holding five 7-second fuses, accessible from the top, and five 15-second fuses, accessible from the bottom. *(Capt W Beeton, Woodbridge Group)*

Nigel Oxenden: "The only real advantage of killing with a knife is that a victim can be lowered and dragged away, rather than collapsing with a clatter of arms and equipment. Considering the relatively few instances of knives actually having been used, they were in danger of becoming weapons of symbolic significance. The knife is perhaps the hardest and noisiest way of killing a conscious man, but is light to carry. Mk3 Fairbairn-Sykes fighting knife *(see also Appendix G).*

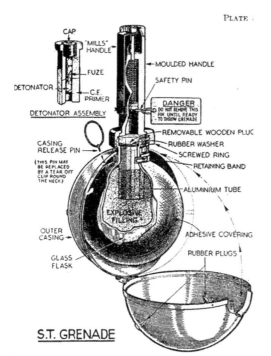

CAP

"MILLS" HANDLE

FUZE

DETONATOR

C.E. PRIMER

DETONATOR ASSEMBLY

MOULDED HANDLE

SAFETY PIN

DANGER
DO NOT REMOVE THIS PIN UNTIL READY TO THROW GRENADE

REMOVABLE WOODEN PLUG

CASING RELEASE PIN
(THIS PIN MAY BE REPLACED BY A TEAR OFF CLIP ROUND THE NECK)

RUBBER WASHER

SCREWED RING

RETAINING BAND

ALUMINIUM TUBE

EXPLOSIVE FILLING

OUTER CASING

ADHESIVE COVERING

GLASS FLASK

RUBBER PLUGS

S.T. GRENADE

Diagram of a Sticky Bomb published in the War Office Training Manual 42:
Tank Hunting and Destruction

The garrotte was the preferred weapon of some auxiliers. Used for centuries as a means of silent assassination, instruction in the use of this deathly weapon is included in the training of many elite military units and Special Forces. Materials used include rope, cable ties, fishing lines, nylon, guitar strings, telephone cord and piano wire. A typical military garrotte consists of two wooden handles attached to a length of flexible wire.

25

John Everett's "tool kit"

The following items were found in John P Everett's (Corporal of Alby Patrol, Norfolk Group 3) "tool kit". (Our thanks go to Shirley, John's widow, for her kind permission to photograph and publish these with John's own descriptions, taken from his memoirs.)

Tin of copper tube igniters - used to put onto Bickford Fuse, ignition of the igniter being by striking it like a match.

Release switch for booby trap use. A percussion cap was fitted into the hole. When fired it ignited an instantaneous fuse (left), and a selection of .45 and long and short .22 rounds.

Pull and pressure switches. Pull switch for trip wires – when sprung it fired off a percussion cap, which in turn ignited a fuse that was attached to it.

Pressure switch. When the button (on the opposite side of the splint seen at bottom right corner) was depressed by the weight of a man or vehicle, it would sever a holding wire and start off a chain of events: fire percussion cap, ignite fuse, and detonate charge.

Pull and pressure switch, and a magnet used to tie explosive onto or mould RDX explosive around, then attach to a metal surface.

The adjuster/anchor end of a trip wire or long garrotte. The wire was wrapped around a tree, strung across the road and wrapped around another tree or post. The adjustor was then used to pull the wire tight and then wrapped over the wire to secure it. *(Source: Stephen Lewins/CART)*

Capt Andrew Croft and "Oxo"

In the summer of 1940, Intelligence Officer Capt (later Colonel) Noel Andrew Croft was instructed to set up Auxiliary Units patrols in East Anglia (Essex, Suffolk and Norfolk). Capt Croft was based at his father's vicarage in the village of Kelvedon in Essex. The first patrols were created in the areas deemed most likely for a German invasion force to land first. Starting in Essex, Capt Croft set out to organise similar units in Suffolk from late July 1940 onwards, progressing steadily northwards up to the region around Framlingham, a market town and civil parish in the Suffolk Coastal District.

Andrew Croft already had a diverse and distinguished career as an Arctic explorer. Together with Lieutenant AST Godfrey and Martin Lindsay he participated in the 1934 British Trans-Greenland Expedition as the expedition photographer and dog handler. In order to do so he learned to speak Danish and Greenlandic, and he also learned to be an expert dog driver. He served as the second-in-command of the Oxford University Arctic Expedition, 1935–36, under the glaciologist AR Glen. The expedition was a 14 month long scientific survey of North-East Land.

After the war, Andrew Croft served as Commandant of the Plymouth-based Infantry Boy's Battalion and the Army Apprentices School at Harrogate. He was later invited to re-create a Cadet Corps for the Metropolitan Police. He is said to have participated in every activity, outdoor and indoor, his example converting new recruits into some of the best policemen of their time. Andrew Croft was awarded the DSO for his achievements in North Africa, Corsica and France during 1943-44 and was appointed OBE in 1970. His participation in the Oxford University Arctic Expedition of 1935-36 earned him the Polar medal. He died in 1998 and his tombstone carries the inscription "Explorer, soldier and leader of men".

When later on in the same year each of the three Counties was appointed its own Intelligence Officer. Norfolk Auxiliary Units came under the command of Capt Nigel Oxenden MC – a cousin of Colonel Gubbins. He was to stay with Auxiliary Units HQ until his retirement in October 1944. Born in London, Capt Oxenden grew up on Jersey to where he returned to after his retirement in order to rebuild the family-run holiday camp at Portelet Bay. During the First World War he was commissioned 2nd Lieutenant and won his MC with bars in 1914 and 1918 respectively. Capt Oxenden served in The Royal Northumberland Fusiliers until he was posted, from 1940 onwards, to various special appointments. By the summer of 1941, Capt Oxenden had left Norfolk to become one of the training officers at Auxiliary Units Headquarters (HQ GHQ Aux Units) at Coleshill House. In 1944, he was asked by the War Office to write a document detailing the official history of the AU, to be deposited in secret military archives. After a prolonged search, conducted by volunteers of the British Resistance Organisation Museum at Parham, Suffolk, the researchers discovered what is believed to be the first typewritten draft of the full document. The original manuscript has never been found and the Ministry of Defence astutely deny ever having set eyes on such a document. In 1998, the draft, titled "Auxiliary Units History and Achievement, 1940 – 1944", was duly published in its original form by 390th Bombardment Group Memorial Air Museum of which the British Resistance Organisation Museum forms a part.

Nigel Oxenden - fondly remembered by his friends and colleagues as "Oxo" - founded the Island Surf Club of Jersey (1923) and he later introduced the technique of "surf-planing" which was hitherto unknown on the island. His surfboard featured a leash, attached to the board by a metal loop on its tail, made from sash window cord that he would tie to his belt - 70 years before the "invention" of the leash. This surfboard is currently on display at the Museum of British Surfing based at Braunton, North Devon. Nigel Oxenden also liked collecting and racing classic motorcycles and cars and he was President of the Jersey Motorcycle and Light Car Club (1943). Major Oxenden died in October 1948, at the age of only 53. In the early 1950s, former members of Norfolk Auxiliary Units patrols under his command arranged for a memorial stone to be placed near his home at Portelet Bay.

Capt G Woodward – formerly the IO for Carmarthen – who stayed in Norfolk until 1943, succeeded Capt Oxenden as Norfolk IO. There was a short period when Norfolk was without an Intelligence Officer of its own – Major RFH Darwall-Smith, who at the time was also IO for Dorset, filled this. According to John Everett, Lieutenant P Pike, formerly of the East Norfolk Scout Section, also served as Norfolk IO, albeit for a short time only.

Norfolk County HQ moved repeatedly, first from Norwich to Beeston Hall and then to Beech House in Wroxham. Yet another home was found at Leicester Square Farm near North Creake, and the final location was at a house near Burnham Market. In Suffolk, Capt JW Holberten was appointed IO in 1941. He was based at Mill House in Cransford near Framlingham, and assisted by Lt Peter Wilkinson and Lt Michael

Henderson. On 4 September 1943, Capt Strangman, the former Intelligence Officer of Somerset Auxiliary Units, replaced Capt Holberten. On 9 February 1944, Capt Holberten in turn replaced Somerset IO Capt JM Martin.

Going to ground – the dugouts

The prototype of a demonstration operational base survives in a thicket in the grounds of Coleshill House. It was accessed through a drop-down entrance shaft that had a rebated blast wall at the bottom. The main chamber, an elephant shelter of Nissen hut-type construction, consisted of a kitchen area, room for six bunks and a cubicle for an Elsan (chemical) toilet. A 'Wendy' (toilet) scheme existed in Norfolk and auxiliers were instructed to "pump ship" (urinate) into the drainpipe rather than into the Elsan "so when you want to rear (defecate) visit drainpipe first"*(see also page 42)*. The emergency escape exit and adjoining tunnel or passageway, commonly found in operational bases all over the counties was, however, replaced by a walk-in entrance, presumably to accommodate a large number of recruits who would have been shown the structure when at Coleshill House for training.

AU patrols' hideouts or OBs, as they were to be called later, were commonly situated in small, out of the way woodlands or copses that enemy troops would be disinclined to investigate too closely. Almost always a footpath or a farm track can be found close by: frequent visits to their base would soon have resulted in the creation of a track, which in turn would have prompted inquisitive passers-by to investigate. Needless to say, this had to be avoided, and for this reason established footpaths or cart tracks were used when ever possible. Favoured locations were riverbanks and disused sand, gravel or marl pits, and occasionally a disused mine, like the one used by the men of Eaton Patrol (Norfolk Group 1). Sand and gravel pits can commonly be found on higher, dry ground and digging into the bank of such a pit is a relatively easy task, whereas heavy clay soil not only indicates wet ground which can be prone to flooding but is also very hard to excavate. Existing structures such as the odd icehouse, farm shed or privy have also occasionally been put to good use.

Although no two OBs are exactly the same, almost all share a number of common characteristics such as a drop-down entrance shaft, a main chamber and an emergency exit passage. Glazed ceramic or unglazed field drain pipes of smaller diameter were frequently used for ventilation. The materials used for building the hideouts varied according to what was available at the time, with bricks, timber and corrugated sheeting being probably the most common. In Norfolk, the first operational bases were rudimentary affairs, constructed from a variety of materials - basically anything that was of use and could be drawn from depleted war supplies. In many cases the cramped conditions within these OBs were due to the scarcity of building materials available. On average the main chambers of operational bases measured 16 by 9 feet. Once equipped with collapsible bunk beds, a stove and a table perhaps surrounded by a few chairs, there was not much room left for six or seven men to move about. Good discipline was paramount *(see page 42)*. For a contemporary list of items frequently kept in OBs *(see page 43)*. The early OBs were commonly built by the patrol members themselves and they often turned out to be uninhabitable, either because of problems with flooding or because of inadequate ventilation, or a combination of both. Castle Rising Patrol (Norfolk Group 8) had to dig a second OB after the candles went out repeatedly and the patrol members almost passed out through lack of oxygen.

Most patrols were soon assisted by Royal Engineers, Auxiliary Units Scout Sections or regular Army and in certain cases even by private builders who were sworn to secrecy.

Improvement arrived with the issue of so-called Mk1 OBs, which were of a more robust design, with the main chamber being an underground Nissen hut-type structure. Commonly referred to as elephant shelters, they were strong and watertight constructions, and easy to set up. Another advantage was that they could be built to fit any required length. The main chamber's interior walls were commonly painted off-white, using white lead paint supplied by military sources (see Appendix C).

OBs that were built by the patrol members themselves sometimes stand out because of their original features, no doubt the work of a patrol member who would have been an expert craftsman. The operational base used by the men of Fundenhall Patrol, for instance, has an emergency escape tunnel that could comfortably be walked along upright. It was built from red brick, taking a zigzag course, and the arched doorways leading off the main chamber all had wooden lintels. Their colleagues from Kirby Bedon Patrol (Norfolk Group 2) made use of an already existing farm shed standing in an isolated location some distance away from the farm. They dug their underground chamber underneath its floor and accessed it through a hatch concealed under the floorboards.

The floor level of an operational base, be it an elephant shelter or a homemade construction, was usually about three metres below ground level and the roof, whether curved or flat, was covered with a thick layer of topsoil that could be up to one metre deep. The construction work was done in utmost secrecy, usually at night or on weekends. Great care was taken not to leave any evidence of recent digging with the spoil being painstakingly removed and deposited elsewhere, where it was less likely to draw attention. Overgrown spoil heaps can occasionally still be found some safe distance away beside a path or on near the edge of a wood. The entrance was usually a drop-down shaft with rungs in one of the walls for access, and an emergency exit, adjoined by a low passage that lead out the opposite way, often in a zigzag course which would protect fleeing patrol members from shrapnel or bullets in the event they would be shot at or that grenades would be thrown into the main chamber. There are, however, a number of operational bases in Norfolk and in Suffolk that do not have an emergency exit. The OBs were stocked with food supplies to last a month and at least some patrols had their own water supplies. Alethorpe Patrol (Norfolk Group 11) stored theirs in four 40-gallon drums, which they had lined up lengthwise against the wall, two on each side, just within the entrance. Other essential items would have been soap, candles, a First Aid kit, a couple of pots and pans, plates and cups, blankets, paraffin stoves and matches. A gallon jug of rum, to be opened in a case of an emergency only, formed part of the standard rations issued and many patrols duly returned their rum untouched at stand-down.

Patrols usually kept a small quantity of ammunition and explosives in their OB. Their main ammunition store, if they had one, was frequently a small, well-hidden dugout some distance away from the operational base. Sometimes a couple of sealed barrels or oil drums buried in the ground served as ammunition store. By the summer of 1941, kits were delivered in improved tin boxes that contained an assortment of stores. A much revised and improved version, with gelignite replacing the formerly issued plastic explosives, was soon to replace "AU Mk1". It was called "Aux Units Mk2" and commonly referred to as a "pack" (see also page 20).

.22 rifles of various patterns, all fitted with silencers and telescopic sights began to also arrive "but long before delivery was complete the telescope was found to be a mistake, adding little to accuracy even when carefully zeroed, and being so easily shifted by handling that ranging shots were always necessary" (N Oxenden). The first of these orders was placed in August 1940 but the perhaps most relevant order was for 660 .22

rifles with silencers fitted, "for Home Guard use". It was placed with Parker-Hale on 13th March 1943. Nigel Oxenden was quite specific about the purpose of the silenced rifles: "These weapons were intended for the sniping of enemy sentries and to fill the larder. In the end they proved their value for competitive training" Documentary evidence, according to which the rifles were to be used for assassinating 5th Columnists and people 'who knew too much' has as yet to be found. Despite this assertion having been made by various auxiliers and despite it being of particular fascination to some historians, it will have to remain speculation until proven. Perhaps the thought was born out of the hysteria regarding enemy spies who were expected to arrive in the country by parachute and the instructions to at least some LDV units that if they were to see the enemy land "to shoot them, shoot them, shoot them without any reference to taking any kind of care of their future" (General Ironside in a speech to senior LDV organisers in York in the first week of June 1940).

Most operational bases were equipped with items of furniture such as a small table and a few chairs, and boards with hooks or nails to hang coats from. Many also contained collapsible bunks for use by the patrol members. Remains of simple bunk beds - wooden frames, boards and wire netting - can be found in some of the OBs, with the best preserved and still in situ probably being in Fritton Lake Patrol's OB on the Norfolk/Suffolk border (Norfolk Group 9).

Patrols frequently set up an observation post (OP) that was situated some 100 to 300 yards distant but within eyesight of the OB. In general, OPs were small, well concealed dugouts covered by corrugated sheeting, like the simple construction used by Sprowston Patrol (Norfolk Group 1) - large enough to accommodate one man, the observer, who would crawl in the shallow depression and remain hidden for hours, to report to his fellow patrol members in the OB, warning of any sightings of enemy troops or other potential dangers via a field telephone.

The OP is officially called the Observer's OB as can be seen in the secret memorandum overleaf. OP and OB were connected via a field telephone line, enabling the observer to communicate with his patrol without having to physically approach the operational base and risk being seen. Stratford St Andrew Patrol (Suffolk Group 3) used the wires of a field fence instead of telephone cable and the men were amazed at how well this worked. Some OPs were constructed in the fashion of hunting seats, nestling high up on a tree, like Woodbridge Patrol's (Suffolk Group 4) lookout post which was situated up an oak tree that afforded wide views across their OB. Others were cleverly hidden within a hollow tree trunk such as Walsingham Patrol's (Norfolk Group 11) or Raydon Patrol's (Suffolk Group 5).

Use of the Observer's O.B. and Telephone.

AU/1

Function of the Observer's O.B.

1.   Firstly, this is to provide a "hide" to enable the observer to go to ground, if the enemy are nearby, and so save the necessity of opening up the Patrol's O.B., which would inevitably disturb its camouflage, and which might jeopardize the lives of the whole Patrol by bringing a closely pursuing enemy on to its O.B.

Secondly, his one man O.B. affords the observer an opportunity to keep in touch with his Patrol by means of the telephone, thereby obviating the necessity for opening up the Patrol O.B. each time he wishes to contact the Patrol Leader. Without the telephone he would be cut off from the latter throughout the hours of daylight.

Thirdly, the one man O.B. forms a Rendezvous for the neighbouring Patrol's message carriers to meet. The whereabouts of Patrol O.Bs. need not therefore be disclosed to personnel of other Patrols. Furthermore, such use of the Observer's O.B. obviates the use of the Call Box method of intercommunication, which is considered hazardous in the extreme, unreliable and a waste of the man power necessary to ensure that messages are not left unfetched for hours or days.

Finally, his O.B. allows the observer an opportunity to take a meal or dress a wound in comparative security. It is emphasized that the Observer's O.B. is NOT intended to be his Observation Post, as it is obvious that their respective character-istics are incompatible, and that a proper observation cannot be carried out from one place alone.

Types and Siting of Observer O.Bs.

2.   These are not restricted to holes in the ground. If broken-down buildings are available, a cellar or demolished room might be adapted. A cluster of really thick bushes is another alternative. Yet another, might be a "slice" cut into the side of a bank, to take a man lying. A bush or undergrowth could be planted on the open side, and Duckboards used for floor and roof.

The essential factors are good camouflage, weatherproof and ease of access.

It is desirable that the Patrol O.B. should be in view of the Observer's O.B., so that the Observer can give warning of enemy presence.

Periscopes.

3.   It is hoped that periscopes may be provided. A hollowed-out tree stump, allowing for the insertion of a periscope, could be planted on the Observer's O.B. lid, thereby giving the Observer a chance of seeing when the coast is clear enough for him to emerge.

Telephones.

4. (a) Issue.

Telephones and cable are being issued on the scale of one pair and half a mile respectively per patrol. The fact that half a mile of wire is allotted per Patrol, does not imply that the Observer's O.B. must be half a mile away. Wire saved on one Patrol might assist in the siting of another Patrol Observer's O.B.

(b)/

33

(b) Wire laying.

The wire should be laid as soon as it is received. For security reasons, the wire which should give a metallic circuit, (i.e. the wire must consist of a double cable, the ends of which are connected to the L1 and L2 terminals of the telephone) must be buried. The line should take a buried path across country covered in undergrowth, or dug along the foot of banks or in ditches. If the wire has to cross roads or tracks, it should pass under bridges or culverts. If it has to pass under water, piping and adhesive tape assist good maintenance.

It is useless fastening wire to tree stumps or bush roots, or leaving it exposed for the wind to remove it from its precarious hold.

The telephone wire should not leave or enter the ground at the O.Bs., but a small tunnel should be bored some five yards away, so that an enemy who may have picked up the wire will come to an abrupt halt a short distance away from the O.B. The tugging of the wire will be noticeable at either end, and necessary drastic action can be taken at short range without delay. The tunnel can be bored by hammering gas piping in a downward direction from the earth's surface to about 2 feet above the floor level of the O.B.

(c) Concealment of Telephone.

A recess should be constructed in the Observer's O.B. to take the telephone. This recess should be covered so that it remains hidden - a board on a hinge is not good enough - a drawer or removable plank, a slat or brick is the best for hiding the recess.

(d) Use of Telephone.

Clear instructions are given inside the lid of each instrument box. Telephones should only be placed into position on "Action Stations", as dampness deteriorates the coils and mechanism.

The telephone should only be adjusted by an experienced person. The Royal Corps of Signals line operator on each I.O's Headquarters will be the competent authority, and he should give elementary instruction on the use of the telephone, when he arrives.

Security.

5.   In case the enemy discover the telephone, a password should precede the conversation. This should be known by all the Patrols within a Group, as messengers from neighbouring Patrols will be wishing to contact Patrol Leaders via the telephone.

In order to prevent the enemy using instruments to discover the telephone lines, the Observer's end should be kept disconnected from the terminal at all times when the telephone is not in use. The Bell dome should be muffled, and the call-up made on the buzzer only.

GHB/PJP

Instructions on the use of an Observer's OB *(observation post, OP)* and telephone.

34

Many Norfolk patrols favoured disused gravel pits for the location for their OB. Earlham Patrol's operational base was located in an old sand pit on the edge of Earlham golf course. The golf course is long gone, replaced by the vast campus of the University of East Anglia. The overgrown pit has been retained as a landscape feature and can be seen at right. No trace remains of the OB.

Glazed ceramic pipes emerging from the ground are good indicators of the presence of an operational base and often they are the only remains still to be found.

Deep crater-like depressions like the one depicted above can be the result of an operational base that was blown up. If the depression is found to be in the "right" location, i.e. near a wood's edge and/or near a path or cart track, chances are that an OB once stood here. Closer investigation of the surrounding ground might lead to the discovery of a shallow gully leading away from it. This would have been the emergency escape exit. Other than that there is usually little else to be found at sites where an OB was blown up. (Site of Happisburgh Patrol's OB in Bacton Wood).

The collapsed roof has revealed the deep layer of topsoil still covering part of Fundenhall Patrol's OB. Note the chimney-like brick-built vent emerging at ground level above the arched entrance doorway.

View from within the main chamber of Mautby Patrol's OB showing part of the roof which has collapsed. The corrugated sheeting seen in the background formed part of the end wall.

Overgrown site of Neatishead Patrol's OB. The roof has long collapsed, leaving a depression in the ground which, over time, has been filled with leaf mould, farm waste and rubbish. A dense growth of brambles makes the site difficult to access.

37

Drop-down entrance shaft at Fritton Lake Patrol's OB *(left)* and the emergency exit opening of West Norfolk Scout Section's OB. In both cases corrugated sheeting was used for lining the earthen walls.

Exposed brickwork on entrance shafts at Holkham Park *(left)* and Fundenhall Patrols' OBs. The top of the entrance shaft of Holkham OB was covered by a crudely applied thick layer of concrete into which, according to some accounts, a hollow tree trunk had been embedded for concealment. The entrance shaft of Fundenhall OB *(right)* was covered by a trap door which too was hidden beneath a hollow tree trunk.

In Suffolk, the first operational bases were built in the area south of Woodbridge. Like further to the north in Norfolk, they were simple dugouts, constructed from a wide variety of materials including disused telegraph poles, railway tracks, railway sleepers and kerbstones.

Debach Patrol's OB is filled with water almost up to its roof.

Herman Kindred, the Stratford St Andrew patrol leader, has given an interesting account, which details how the place for their operational base was chosen and also how it was built.

"At the end of October 1940 the engineers (Royal Engineers) were ready to build our hideout. I rather objected to the location they had chosen because I thought if we dig down there we have a clay substance and we are going to have a big water problem here. They had another rethink and they asked me to have another look around the area and maybe make a suggestion as to where a better location could be found."

The men did indeed find a more suitable location further towards the east and the Royal Engineers eventually selected the site that had been suggested to them by the patrol members. They were also going to try to make good use of the nearby A12 road and build an observation post there.

"They put our shell down and very well done it was. The work and all the camouflaging was very quickly done. I think they said that if anything happened, that if anybody asked what was going on, to say that an emergency food supply store was going to be put up for the village. That was the tale given out by the Army at the time."

Stratford St Andrew Patrol's stores were kept in a passage that ran off the far end of their operational base. Herman Kindred explains:

"In this tunnel we placed our stores. We kept our explosives in one compartment; in the next one would be food and water etc and probably paraffin oil as well. In the next one we kept our detonator equipment. It was a golden rule that detonators should never be kept anywhere near the explosives."

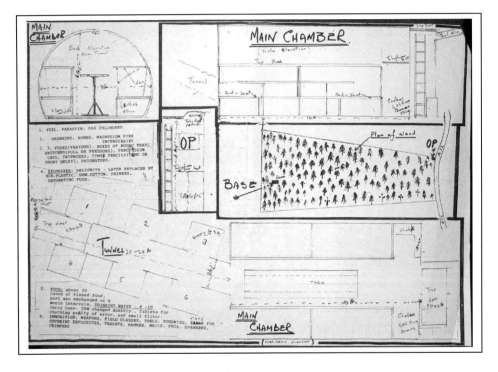

Drawing depicting Stratford St Andrew Patrol's dugout and observation post, with some additional information typed in, created by Herman Kindred. (*Archived at the British Resistance Organisation Museum, Parham, Suffolk*)

A walk-in replica of Stratford St Andrew Patrol's OB, including the tunnel used for storage, can be visited at the near-by British Resistance Organisation Museum which adjoins the control tower at the former Parham airfield.

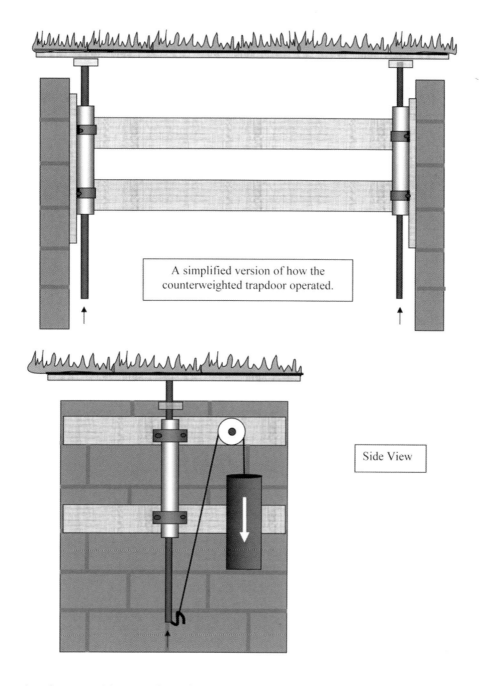

A simplified version of how the
counterweighted trapdoor operated.

Side View

Drawing of counterweight-assisted trap door mechanism. This design is known to have been used at operational patrols' OBs as well as at Special Duties Branch wireless IN- Station dugouts. *(See Norwich IN-Station, p 170)*

                    R U L E S.

1. Put Food Scraps in tins and put lids on.

2. Put all other refuse, including paper, in zinc box.
      (Stamp out cig. ends first)

3. Rear in El-san.

   Pump-ship in Drain-pipe

            (So when you want to rear, visit drain-pipe first)
4. Put waste water down Drain-pipe.

5. Put all blankets in Bin immediately on getting up.

   Put great-coats in other Bin.

6. Store Bread and rowls in trunk.

7. ANTI-FIRE
            1. Keep spades handy at 3 different points to
               shovel sand over burning material.

            2. If blankets are on fire either smother with
               other blankets or put in bin, if empty.

            3. Requisition Fire-extinguisher.

            4.

8. BUNKS. 2 blankets per man, great-coats, and cover with
   ground-sheet except on lower bunk.

9. WATCH-KEEPING.

      Take temperature-readings hourly during day and until
      01.00 hrs, thereafter at 2 hour intervals.

RECREATION	TRAINING	JOBS
1. Darts	1. Map-reading	1. Cooking
2. Radio	2. Calendar Revision	2. Washing-up.
3. Cards	3. Message Writing	3. Instalment of Drain-pipe.
4. Reading.		4. Bracket for Lamp.
		5. Shelves
		6. Chimney for El-san.
		7. Baffle-board for Ventilator
		8. Arrange tins for food scraps.

It is of interest to note that this document concerning OB maintenance and discipline uses two terms of Navy slang -"Rear in Elsan" and "Pump-ship in drainpipe"- referring to defecation and urination. This is evidence of the instructions having indeed originated from a report issued by the Royal Navy's Submarine Testing Station, extracts of which were distributed to AU patrols by Norfolk IO, Capt G Woodward, on 7 October 1942. Under 'Hygiene' the paper clearly states that 'Elsan must be used for evacuation of faeces only. For urination tins or bottles with screw caps should be used.

To take:

1. Bread (4 loaves)
2. Lard (6 oz)
3. Bread Knife
4. Dart Board.
5. Slippers.
6. Matches.
7. Torch.
8. Dish Cloth.
9. Meth.Spirit.
10. 1 or 2 Russets
11. Blankets. (10)
12. Primus
13. Prickers
14. Cake.
15. Cigarettes
16. Funnel
17. Water-bottle (full)
18. Water Purifier.
17. Towel
18. Maps.
19. Alarm Clock.
20. Mantle
21. Cheese

PAPERS
1 'Wendy' papers
Calendars
Notepaper
Blotting-paper
Envelopes.
Marks papers.
Log-Book (Patrol)
          (Wendy)
Books if any (Short Story)
          W.W.Jacobs
Petrol Claims
Subsistence Forms
Cinema Memoranda.
Diary.

A list of items one of the Norfolk AU patrols kept in their operational base. The men used a Primus stove for cooking and had books and a dartboard for entertainment. They had blankets and slippers, a cake and some cheese for comfort, as well as cigarettes. They had even thought of bringing an alarm clock. "1 'Wendy' papers" means one roll of toilet paper. The last item on the list is a diary. Sadly, only very few diaries kept by patrol members have found their way into a museum collection.

43

Counterweights that would once have helped move the heavy trapdoors at Sibton Patrol's OB

1940s Valor paraffin stove *(left)* and other paraphernalia at Wangford Patrol's OB

Auxiliary Units operational patrols in Norfolk

By 1941, a total of 201 men had been recruited in Norfolk, forming 11 groups divided into 35 patrols. 40 operational bases had been built and eight more were planned. By 1942, the number of men recruited and active in Norfolk Auxiliary Units patrols had increased to 276 and the number of patrols amounted to 45.

The Norfolk, AU patrols were divided into groups numbered from 1 through to 11. Each one of the groups consisted of a number of Auxiliary Units patrols, ranging from two to six, and was contained within a (sometimes very roughly) defined geographical area in which the patrols operated. With stretches of country without any suitable men available however, it was inevitable that some scattered patrols did not fall naturally into these groups.

Norfolk Group 10, for instance, was made up of five patrols. However, only three of the group's patrols were based in the South Norfolk - North Suffolk border area near Brandon, Lakenheath and Hockwold - close to the county boundaries of Norfolk, Suffolk and Cambridgeshire. The other two patrols in Group 10 were 25 and 30 miles away, respectively, with one having been based near Fakenham and the other near East Dereham in the Breckland district, both in North Norfolk. Two of the four men assisting GCO Capt Walter G Gentle, who lived in Brandon, came from the Fakenham/East Dereham area, and were hence in an ideal position to look after the group's two scattered patrols.

The other extreme, as it were, can be found along the north coast of Norfolk - an area extending for about 35 kilometres (22 miles), as the crow flies, from Hunstanton in the west to Cromer in the east, where records reveal the presence of only two patrols (in Norfolk Group 6): Brancaster and Holkham Park Patrols.

Some of the patrols were known or referred to under different names, names that could have originated from the patrol leader's home village or from the village the majority of members came from, from the largest village in the area or from the general location their operational base was located in. Some of the names have no immediately obvious link at all. It is understood that at least some patrols also had a code name.

To complicate matters further, auxiliers who all were members of the same patrol sometimes use different names: one might be calling it "Alby" Patrol (Norfolk Group 3) whereas another would be referring to it as "Calthorpe" Patrol and a third might know it as "Thorpe Market" Patrol. The same situation applies to a number of Suffolk patrols. Presumably a name did not mean much to any of them because they, after all, knew who they were and where they were going. Trying to establish which was which 70 years later is quite another matter.

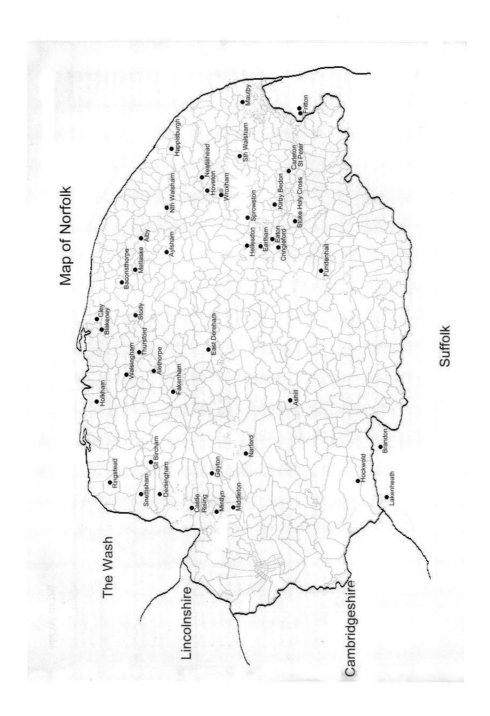

Map of Norfolk

The Wash

Lincolnshire

Cambridgeshire

Suffolk

Mautby
Fritton
Happisburgh
Sth Walsham
Neatishead
Carleton
St Peter
Nth Walsham
Hoveton
Wroxham
Kirby Bedon
Sprowston
Stoke Holy Cross
Alby
Aylsham
Helesdon
Eaton
Earlham
Cringleford
Baconsthorpe
Matlaske
Fundenhall
Cley
Blakeney
Stody
Thursford
East Dereham
Walsingham
Alethorpe
Fakenham
Holkham
Ashill
Narford
Ringstead
Gt Bircham
Gayton
Brandon
Snettisham
Dersingham
Hockwold
Castle
Rising
Mintlyn
Middleton
Lakenheath

NORFOLK GROUP 1 (Norwich)

GCO Capt RW Eades,
replaced by Lt CH Buxton, assisted by Sgt J Page

Lt Buxton left AU following a training accident witnessed by Earlham Patrol member George Gibbs:

> "It happened in the quarry in Whitlingham Lane. We were learning about unit charges and how to detonate them. We had made up about a half dozen charges and Lt Buxton said fuse them to any object you like. They had ½-hour fuses attached and we duly retired and after half an hour about four of the charges had exploded and as it was frosty Lt Buxton said 'maybe they delayed a bit' and after 5 to 10 minutes he said 'I'll have to go and see what's gone wrong'. A minute after he had entered the quarry one of the charges exploded. We went in and Lt Buxton was on the ground bleeding profusely from his face. It was a mask of blood and we carried him out and got an ambulance and he was rushed to hospital. I can't remember seeing Lt Buxton again. The unit charge had been fused to a large flint stone and it had disintegrated and dozens of pieces of flint had entered his face."

Eaton Patrol: Sgt Fred G Matthews; Cpl HF Lambert; Pte TR Foulger; Pte D Cozens; Pte RV Creed

The patrol's OB was located in Harford Hills Mine, a disused chalk mine situated down a quiet lane and off the beaten track. A number of chalk and flint workings are known to have existed beneath the city of Norwich and its southern suburbs, with collapsing mine tunnels and shafts occasionally creating large holes (and ensuing traffic chaos) in the city's streets. Harford Hills Mine, like all others, has long since closed and the area was transformed into a local nature reserve. For health and safety reasons the entrance into the mine, which has a system of tunnels measuring altogether about one kilometre in length, is being kept sealed. A corrugated iron pipe of about four feet (1.20 m) in diameter lines the first few metres of the entrance leading into the main tunnel - although not used very often, this type of pipe is documented as having been used in damp locations. Crawl spaces and larger passages turn off the main tunnel in various directions along the way, their walls bearing the soot marks made by candles. The mine is stable, dry and well ventilated and the warren of tunnels provided not only escape routes but also many places where the men could have hidden themselves in case their hideout was discovered.

When not engaged in night operations at their OB, the patrol members went to Whitlingham sand pits for rifle and Tommy gun practice or they went to fire-fighting training at Newmarket Road in Norwich – probably because Home Guard were trained in winter 1940/41 to support Civil Defence in fire fighting after major enemy raids. They attended explosives courses held at Wroxham, presumably tutored by members of the AU Scout Section patrol based at Beech House, and they conducted mock attacks on the aerodromes located near St Faith and at Feltwell. Their training also included climbing the steep sides of the pits at Whitlingham with their gas masks on, and of course they went on a weekend training course at Coleshill House.

Evidence suggests that patrol leader Sgt Matthews was one of a group of men attached to No. 62 Commando, who, on the night of 3 October 1942 were involved in "Operation Basalt", a raid on the island of Sark during which several prisoners were shot and left dead on the beach and Sgt Matthews lost one of his hands.

Earlham Patrol: Sgt CG Haines; Cpl SA Haines; Pte RG Bailey; Pte F Brown; Pte BC Claxton; Pte JG Fish; Pte JE Walker; Pte John Fielding

Earlham Patrol's OB was built by the patrol member themselves. It has been described as having consisted of a main chamber measuring 3.70 x 2.50m, with an entrance passage, a central area for bunks, and an explosives store. It was situated on the north-eastern edge of Earlham golf course. The golf course no longer exists, with the land having been built over by the Sainsbury Centre of Visual Arts and the University of East Anglia in the 1950s. Nothing remains of the OB site but the disused pit it was built into has been retained as a landscape feature on the university campus.

Sgt CG Haines recalls:

> "I was an engineer at Laurence Scott and in a reserved occupation at the time. I had been in the Army Cadets and had done quite a lot of boxing. I was 26 years old when I was approached by someone who was already a member. When I was recruited I had to tell my family that I was in a local anti-tank unit."

An excerpt from John Fielding's 1942 diary gives a glimpse of the patrol's activities in what would have been a busy year for the men. The diary is also evidence of a blatant breach of security: auxiliers were not supposed to know the whereabouts of other OBs so they could not give them away to the enemy in case they were caught and tortured.

January
8 – Parade at Earlham OB
13 – See Turner about duty *(Capt Percy Ernest Turner, see Appendix D)*
20 – At Earlham OB

February
8 – Collect rifles and revolvers from Veterans Club *(Princes Street, Norwich)*
15 – Tunnel caved in but mended very satisfactorily
22 – Meet Turner to go to OB and collect corrugated iron

March
1 - Rifle shooting at Whitlingham sandpits
5 – Take car to Beeston with others to see Capt Woodward *(Beeston Hall HQ)*
6 – Woodward gives general lecture at Veterans Club
15 – Pick up others to go to Whitlingham for Tommy gun firing
18 – Night patrol at Cringleford OB
23 – NCOs meeting at Veterans Club
29 – Earlham OB inspection by Capt Woodward
30 – Marston Lane night patrol

April
1 – Patrol at Sprowston OB
5 – Cringleford OB inspected by Capt Woodward

Private John Fielding later joined the SAS and he was one of the eight lucky men who survived "Operation Bulbasket" – an ill-fated operation conducted by SAS B Squadron behind German lines in German-occupied France. Thirty-four of his colleagues, a number of them ex-auxiliers and AU Scout Section patrol members, were executed by German troops and buried in a mass grave in the woods. They were later re-interred in the village cemetery of Rom, Deux-Sèvres.

Sprowston Patrol: Sgt RL Wright; Cpl JD Thorne; Pte HP Bowman; Pte ER Higgs; Pte JE Smith; Pte JA Ridgway; Pte F Taylor; Pte Harold Wm Parker

The patrol's operational base is an extensive affair consisting of an elephant shelter with tunnels to an ammunition store and an escape tunnel, situated in a privately owned wood comprising conifers and deciduous trees.

The OB site presents itself as three pronounced depressions in the ground. The smallest of these was caused by the collapse of the drop-down entrance shaft at the eastern end of the main chamber, which is an elephant shelter. A section of roof is still in place, supported by the end wall, forming a cave-like shelter underneath which has been partially filled in with rubble in order to prevent access for local children who used to play there. The remaining roof has collapsed, forming a second, larger, roughly square-shaped depression.

A passageway, now collapsed, lead at right angles from the western end of the main chamber to the ammo store, located approx 25 metres distant and connected by a tunnel. It had a flat roof supported by lengths of telegraph poles resting on wooden uprights and was covered with corrugated sheeting.

Patrol member HP Bowman recalls:

> "I joined the Home Guard as a young apprentice and then, one day, I was called into the Commander's office at the Drill Hall located by Chapelfield Gardens in Norwich. A panel of officers asked me a lot of questions starting with my age. I said "16, no, I mean 18"... We were specially trained in sabotage skills and one of our exercises involved getting through airfield security at Rackheath airfield and then symbolically blowing up planes. Another part of our training was in unarmed combat which we practiced in a field behind a Norwich school. Jack Ridgeway, who had taken a 'Mr Atlas' course, took this class. No one could outfight him but he taught us a few tricks."

An interesting account given by Mr Neil Evans, a local resident, was published by Chris Bird *(in: Silent Sentinels, 1999):*

> "The Norwich base, in Belmore Plantation, off South Hill Road, had three rooms, connected by a long passageways. There were two entrance hatches. The complex was just below ground level, covered with soil and pine needles. To give ventilation, some pine trees were cut down to their stumps, which were then hollowed out. Mr Evans stumbled across the Norwich base in 1946, finding some hand grenades inside, about which he notified the police."

The patrol also had an observation post the remains of which can still be seen. It was a simple rectangular dugout, presumably covered with corrugated sheeting.

Members of Group 1 (Norwich) patrols: Back row from left: Unknown – unknown - Ernest F Roxby
Front row from left: Arthur W Roxby – FG Matthews of Eaton Patrol – unknown – unknown – HF
'Darkie' Lambert of Eaton Patrol *(Picture taken in 1942, source: Russell Roxby)*

Very little is known about the other two patrols in Group 1 - Hellesdon Patrol and
Cringleford Patrol. Both patrols are mentioned and joint activities with the other patrols
in the group described in some detail in John Fielding's diary (written in 1942) but some
of the patrol members' names as well as their operational bases have as yet to be found.
The names of nine men only have been documented but to which patrol they belonged
could not be established with certainty. Their postal addresses indicate that the men
would in all likelihood have been members of Hellesdon Patrol. Records show that
some were returned to their local Home Guard in January 1944, in other words, at least
one but in all probability both Hellesdon and Cringleford Patrols were disbanded before
stand-down. Names possibly associated with Hellesdon Patrol are: George Gibbs
(returned to HG 31 Jan 1944); Robert Thomas Maskell (returned to HG 31 Jan 1944);
Raymond Edward Woods (returned to HG 31 Jan 1944); Ernest Frederick Roxby
(returned to HG 31 Jan 1944); AW Roxby; FE Blythe; RC Cooper; AS Bird; PAA Hawes
(died 12 Nov 1943)

Cringleford Patrol: Some reshuffling appears to have been done in Norwich Group.
In his 1942 diary, auxilier John Fielding (Earlham Patrol) mentions altogether five
patrols but only three appear in official lists. According to the diary, John Fielding and
his patrol members were busy building or repairing their OB at the Earlham site, only
about one kilometre distant from the Cringleford location. The Cringleford OB was

50

located in a privately owned wood near Keswick Hall, at what appears to be the highest elevation in the vicinity. A crater-like depression remains, with pieces of broken concrete and old bricks scattered around its perimeter. A metal detector survey revealed that a lot of metal is still in the ground, most of it around the perimeter. We concluded from this that in all likelihood the OB was blown up so as not to give away its purpose - at the time AU would still have been active. Considering the fact that the patrol and their OB are mentioned in John Fielding's diary - proof that it did indeed exist, for some time at least - the most plausible explanation for it not being listed in official documents is that the patrol was disbanded before stand-down. Auxiliers who lived in the vicinity and whose names might be associated with this patrol are RG Bailey, F Brown, BC Claxton, JG Fish and JE Walker, but this information has yet to be verified.

No. 28 Newmarket Road, Eaton (Norwich) served as the first Norfolk Auxiliary Units HQ

NORFOLK GROUP 2

GCO Capt HWR Mitchell, Kirby Bedon

Carleton St Peter Patrol: Sgt Frederick John Brewington (post master); Cpl Sidney Hubert James Saxton (fruit grower); Pte William Ernest; Pte Thomas William Trett (farm worker); Pte William Herbert Alderton (milk roundsman)

The patrol members came from the villages of Rockland St Mary and Claxton, located a couple of miles further down the road to Langley Street. The patrol's operational base has as yet to be found.

Fundenhall Patrol: Sgt R Bothway (farmer); Cpl P Myhill (farm worker); Pte DG Warman (farm worker); Pte J Moore (farm worker); Pte Lenny Lawn (farm worker); Pte Jack Gamble (farm manager); Pte Edward Dring (estate manager)

The patrol was sometimes also referred to as Ashwellthorpe Patrol. The patrol members themselves built their OB, mainly on Sunday mornings. It was an elephant shelter with a brick-built drop-down entrance shaft that was hidden under a hollow tree trunk. Single bricks had been set endways on into one wall of the shaft, serving as steps. A short passage, with a roof supported by timber, lead from the bottom of the shaft into the main chamber. The doorways leading off the main chamber had wooden lintels and rounded arches, and they were set in walls built from red brick. A brick-built vent still emerges from above the entrance doorway.

Contained in the vent was a length of galvanised pipe that carried the wire used to suspend the counterweight for the entrance hatch. When pulled, the wire released the catch that opened the hatch. Part of the main chamber has collapsed but it is possible to get a glimpse of the brick wall at the far end. Unusually, behind the exit doorway is a narrow passage which is as high as the roof of the main chamber would have been before it collapsed. The passage has brick walls and sturdy roof timbers. Taking a dogleg course, space for a toilet cubicle was made in the bend. The emergency exit opening, now backfilled with soil and leaf mould, terminates in the bank of a small pond or marl pit. The OB was used for storing ammunition, explosives and various other items of equipment. The men never slept in it. All ammunition was removed and the phosphorous grenades blown up at the end of the war.

The patrol members attended two meetings per week held at the Drill Hall in Wymondham and they paraded as well as drilled and received weapons training on weekends. Many weekends, lasting from Friday to Sunday, were spent at Leicester Square Farm, where they were trained by special Army units. Duties during the week included testing security at searchlight units and other military establishments based in the area.

Patrol member Jack Gamble recalls:

"I was the manager of Wattlefield estate and in a reserved occupation and was hence unable to join the regular forces. However, I did join the Home Guard and then one day, out of the blue, a friend asked me if I would like to be transferred to another branch of the Home Guard. He was unable to tell me what it was about, but said it was very interesting. In due course I joined 202 Battalion...Our training was intensive and on many weekends, from Friday to Sunday... One of our raids was on a military arsenal outside Norwich. We tried to gain information by listening to conversations in pubs, without success. The raid was a failure and we were all captured."

Patrol member DG Warman remembers:

"Our unit had its own car. It was a Wolseley and two of us had to sit on a plank of wood at the back."

Kirby Bedon Patrol: Sgt W Eke; Cpl E Reeve; Pte A Brown; Pte H (MJ?) Cracknell; Pte RJ Ewles; Pte BJ Rix

Certainly one of the more unusual locations for an OB, the patrol members had theirs dug below an isolated shed that was used for storing apple boxes and crates in one of the extensive orchards of The Grange. The operational base was accessed through a trapdoor in the floor which opened to a drop-down shaft, with a short passage leading into the main chamber. The hideout did not have an emergency exit. The Grange was razed to the ground after the war and no trace remains of the patrol's operational base, although its position has been identified.

Stoke Holy Cross Patrol: Sgt WA "Dickie" Bickerson; Cpl Harry "Pitman" W Lynes; Pte GR Allen; Pte Roy Benjamin "Dick" Allen (farm worker); Pte Geoffrey Arthur E Newman; Pte John E Sayer; Pte SG Sexton; Pte PA Winterbone (farmer)

Nothing but a shallow depression in the ground marks the spot where the operational base had stood, in an area on Skeet's Hill, near disused sand and gravel pits that were regularly frequented by the patrol's members for target practice. The elevated location offered wide views of the surrounding countryside.

A pipe made from corrugated sheeting lines the entrance to Harford Hills Mine. The warren of tunnels provided a safe and dry haven for the men of Eaton Patrol. AU operational units in other Counties such as in Devon or Cornwall commonly used disused mines and this type of entrance tunnel has been documented from some OBs in Northumberland. A number of old chalk mines can be found in the vicinity of Norwich, creating dangerous holes in busy city roads when the roof of one collapses. For health and safety reasons Harford Hills Mine, parts of which are situated below an adjoining golf course, is not usually accessible to the public although experts still consider it stable and safe. It is the only such location used by a Norfolk patrol.

Old pot, in situ near the end of the main tunnel at Harford Hills Mine.

The brick-built emergency exit passage *(left)* with its arched doorway and wooden lintel *(right)* at Fundenhall Patrol's OB. The walls were painted white to make it easier for the men to find their way by candlelight.

An overgrown sand and gravel pit on Skeet's Hill - the site of Stoke Holy Cross Patrol's OB

Site of Sprowston Patrol's OB

The remains of Sprowston Patrol's observation post.

NORFOLK GROUP 3

GCO Capt George Milton Duncan OBE
assisted by Lt Peter Norris Neave (miller and farmer in Felmingham).

They were joined at a later date by Sgt A George Abel, Aylsham Patrol leader, who worked as secretary for a local insurance company in Aylsham for many years.

Alby Patrol: Sgt Alec Scott (farmer); Cpl John Philip Everett (farmer); Pte GH "John" Wosternholme; Pte David Mackie/MacKay; Pte Leonard Daniels; Pte Raymond "Timmy" Buller (joined later); Pte Max Cremer (joined later)

Like a number of Norfolk patrols, the men from Alby patrol favoured a disused sandpit for the location of their operational base. It was located in a private wood off a quiet country lane and they built it themselves from corrugated sheeting and wood. They had paraffin lighting, iron rations and a medical kit. Their nearby explosives store, amongst various other explosives and incendiary devices, contained a number of phosphorous bombs, as well as slabs of gun cotton which the auxiliers intended to use for sabotaging railway lines. They already had a plan in place, should the enemy ever arrive in their area. A specific part of the Cromer to Norwich line, where it passed through the land they patrolled, had been chosen for the placing of explosives to cause the maximum inconvenience to the enemy.

The stretch of line chosen was the cutting between Tylers Bridge and Gunton station. John Everett explains:

> "Blowing up railway lines and derailing trains in a cutting posed particular problems to those carrying out a repair, in that the bent lines had to be removed from the cutting, and much more importantly, the removal of the derailed train. To do this same sabotage work on an embankment would allow both bent line and derailed train to be toppled down the embankment by the repair crew."

After the initial supply of arms, ammunition and equipment had been received, further supplies would be delivered to Capt Duncan's bungalow in Cromer Road, North Walsham, where the area quartermaster, Mr Alfred Barrett, would sign them out to the individual patrols. He and Mr Barrett would then deliver these, including explosives, in Capt Duncan's car. They would also take stores from the OB if they were out of date or required replacement. Interestingly, the patrol had their own secret "dead letter box" where messages could be dropped. It was located at the foot of a telegraph pole close to the OB.

The men were equipped with Smith & Wesson revolvers and they had an American Lewis machine gun, which they shared. They were trained in the use of explosives by Army specialists two or three times a week. It is uncertain if the elephant shelter was removed after the war or whether it has collapsed. Apart from shards of glazed ceramic pipes littering the site no trace remains of the OB.

Patrol member Max Cremer recalls:

> "When the Government appealed for volunteers to join the Home Guard, I enrolled at Erpingham village hall. I was issued with an old .300 American rifle to train with. Later, I was asked by a Capt Bray if I would volunteer to join an underground movement (202 Battalion) which would be trained in the use of explosives ... at the time it was believed that the Germans might land on the North Norfolk coast."

Aylsham Patrol: Sgt A George Abel; Cpl Jack Hamilton Dye (gamekeeper); Pte Thomas George Bailey; Pte Arthur John Clarke; Pte Donald Jack Lee; Pte HJ Stickells; Pte Victor Wells

None of the men from Aylsham patrol appear to ever have talked publicly about their activities with Auxiliary Units and hence the site of their operational base, situated in private wood on the Blickling Estate, has only recently been found. The OB appears to have (at least partially) collapsed, indicated by a fairly large shallow depression in the ground. A small part of the upper rim of the elephant shelter's roof has been exposed by burrowing animals, the area immediately behind it appears to be filled with soil up to the roof.

One of the patrol members who wished to remain anonymous recalls:

> "Our training was frequent, professional and always at night. We always wore Home Guard uniform and as far as the rest of the Home Guard were concerned we were part of the Home Guard...During a training exercise held in the Midlands two of us were in a dugout with a live grenade each. I threw mine but my colleague dropped his with the lever 'on'. Well, the lever fell out but I picked it up and threw it out of the dugout... We were trained to act as guerrillas in the event of a German invasion... At the end of the war we had lots of ammunition and explosives to dispose of, we were told to remove the detonators, put it underground and burn it."

Baconsthorpe Patrol: Sgt John George Seaman (farmer); Cpl Donald Llewellyn "Steve" Daglish; Pte JF Rix (discharged); Pte Anthony Smith (he replaced Rix); Pte Hedley George Smith; Pte Harry Paul Adlard (discharged pre Sept 1942); Pte Archibald Albert Newstead

Of all the Auxiliary Units patrols in Norfolk, the men from Baconsthorpe Patrol had chosen by far the grandest location for their OB: it was built into the base of one of the towers in the curtain wall surrounding Baconsthorpe Castle. By the 1940s, however, this fine fortified manor house had already fallen into disrepair and its remains were badly overgrown, with shrubs and trees almost completely covering the ruins and dense vegetation growing in the surrounding moat – an ideal hiding place.

An Anderson shelter was placed into the base of the north-west tower. It was a tight fit. The OB was completely sealed off, with the only way in (and out) being a narrow crawlspace that patrol members had dug under the adjoining wall. This crawlspace can still be seen. The castle has since been taken into the care of English Heritage who have designated it a Grade I listed building and a Scheduled Ancient Monument. The Anderson shelter was removed after the war and no physical trace remains of the operational base. There is one small item, though: an auxilier might well have put a rusty nail in the tower's exterior east wall where it can still be seen.

The patrol trained on four nights per week and the men attended extra weekend training courses at Leicester Square Farm, at Holt and on the firing ranges at Plumstead Heath.

Patrol leader Sgt John George Seaman was a well-liked and well-known character who had farmed in the area for 70 years. After joining the Territorial Army he became a small arms instructor with the 5th Battalion Royal Norfolk Regiment. He returned to farming in 1943 and soon became involved with AU, replacing DL Dalglish as the patrol leader. After the war Mr Seaman built a combination seed drill and he also designed a side-mounted tractor bale loader. He judged Holt & District Farmers' Club ploughing matches for 40 years and remained a keen sportsman well into his eighties.

Matlaske Patrol: Sgt Henry West (Little Barningham); Pte D Thaxter; Pte W Seaman; Pte A Roper; Pte Leonard Youngs; Pte Robert Bix (Little Barningham); Pte L Daniels (transferred); Pte B Grubb

The patrol's operational base was situated in close proximity of a sand and gravel extraction site, in a small private wood that is adjoined by fields on two sides. A quiet country lane skirts the wood, and a farm track leads past only a short distance away.

The structure appears to have been removed at quite some time ago but the site still is clearly marked by a deep depression. It is believed that the patrol members themselves built the OB. The main chamber is described as having been a Nissen hut-type structure with corrugated sheeting, held in place by a timber frame, lining the earthen end walls. Judging from the large and pronounced depression left in the ground it would in all likelihood have been a standard sized elephant shelter.

Some 100 metres further to the south-east the remains of the patrol's ammunition store can still be seen. It was a rectangular dugout measuring approximately one by two metres. Its depth can no longer be established due to soil and leaf mould having gradually filled in the hole over the decades. Some of the corrugated sheeting lining the walls is still in situ, as are several corrugated sheets that would once have formed the roof. The overgrown spoil heap can be seen a short distance away.

An excerpt taken from Sgt Henry West's diary allows a glimpse of the patrol's activities during the summer of 1942:

June 2nd	Hand grenade practice
June 6th/7th	Coleshill Competition
June 9th	Weekly Meeting at OB
June 16t	Tommy gun practice for relay race
June 21st	Practice for second round of competition
June 28th	Group meeting at Cawston
June 30th	Hand grenade practice

The following snippets were taken from pencilled notes jotted down in his diary by Sgt Henry West in 1944 on occasion of a trip to the Isle of Wight, where men from several patrols in Group 3 - Baconsthorpe, Alby, Matlaske and North Walsham – were involved:

"We travelled in a spacious 3rd class carriage and were collected at Liverpool Street station by an Army truck that took us across London to Waterloo station, where we had to wait for the connecting train to Portsmouth. Whilst we were waiting, the air raid warning siren went off and then we heard a loud bang. GCO Lt Neave informed us that a robot plane (V1, Doodlebug) having crashed had caused it. After our arrival in Portsmouth we went straight down to the harbour and saw invasion barges and also HMS Warspite, which looked quite battered. In the evening of the same day we got on board of a big launch that took us to the Isle of Wight. We were taken to Newport in Army trucks and reported to headquarters at Billingham Manor, where the food was good and the beds decent.

The following day we went to Sandown on duty. We were inspected by the Colonel and had a long lecture on the shortage of troops on the island. We were put up at the Sandringham Hotel, three in a room. We visited Shanklin, a famous holiday resort in peacetime, and took walks along the cliff paths, and we also went to the pictures to see "Northern Pursuit", "Angels Sing" and "Nancy Drew Detective"."

Sgt West notes that although the soil seemed poor there were roses everywhere, and also that the island was full of children and that one couldn't help seeing how clean and healthy they looked.

One of their party was Alby Patrol's corporal, John Everett, and he too remembers the trip:

"From Ryde Pier we were taken to Newport and then split up and allocated various duties. I was to go with the Welsh Borderers to be stationed at the village of Freshwater. Soon members of the Durham Miners Auxiliary Units were to join our patrol. On D Day, I clearly saw part of the invasion fleet leave the Solent and later heard the bombing and shelling of the Normandy beaches. I could see the palls of smoke on the horizon together with the aircraft and ships going and coming from France to England.

The task given to all these mish-mash of auxiliers on the Isle of Wight was to form anti-invasion patrols in case of a German counter attack. After three weeks we were relieved of our duties on the island and replaced by others."

Picture taken by an Isle of Wight auxilier at Freshwater, Isle of Wight - from left to right:
Sgt Henry West (Matlaske patrol leader), Lt Peter Neave (GCO Norfolk Group 3), Pte Robert Bix (Matlaske Patrol), Sgt George Abel (Aylsham patrol leader), Cpl John Everett (Alby Patrol)
(Photo source: John and Shirley Everett)

Stody Patrol: Sgt Albert Edward High; Sgt William Davies (he was killed in an accident) - replaced by Sgt Jack C High (estate worker); Pte Fred Andrews (farm manager); Pte William Kendle Emery (estate worker); Pte Ernest Robert Hazelwood; Pte Harold Ernest Sewell (estate worker) – he was replaced by Pte Wallace "Carol" Shayler (estate worker) who was assigned his registration number

Stody Patrol was composed mainly of men who worked for the Stody Estate. Like many of their colleagues they had built their OB in a disused sand pit without the help from Royal Engineers. The main chamber had a curved corrugated iron roof and was later enlarged at the rear to accommodate an explosives store. The walls seem to have been lined with what appears to be carpet underlay or felt (presumably to keep out dampness), held in place with wire netting and then covered with corrugated sheeting. The hide was accessed by a ladder down a drop-down shaft which was lined with corrugated sheeting and covered with a trap door.

The OB had no emergency exit. A 3-inch water pipe provided some ventilation. Patrol members were sometimes ordered to spend weekends in the OB to acclimatise themselves and they were always glad to leave on Sundays to get some fresh air. The structure has since silted up and the roof is partially collapsed.

An observation post was situated within sight of the OB. It consisted of a dugout that was covered with corrugated sheeting and well camouflaged. The OP had a field telephone connection with the OB.

The patrol's main target was the LNER (London and North Eastern Railway) line and the nearby railway works at Melton Constable. The patrol's training consequently concentrated on disrupting and blowing up railway lines and they had sections of railway track on which to practise.

Private HE Sewell was called up in May 1944. He joined the Suffolk Regiment and went to Bury St Edmunds for basic training. He later moved into a Welsh Regiment before being sent to Germany. He was in Hamburg on the day Germany surrendered and Peace was declared. Mr Sewell then served in the MPs for the following three years and returned to his Norfolk home with a German wife.

North Walsham Patrol: Sgt Fredrick Kidman; Cpl Frank Nicholas Tofts; Pte Thomas John Bell; Pte Wallace Charles Hannant; Pte William Alma Hicks; Pte Alfred Barrett (he was later promoted to Group 3 Quartermaster)

This is another patrol which built their operational base without the assistance of Royal Engineers. They set about their task in the yard of Heath Farmhouse, Corporal Tofts' home. From there it was carted across the field to the OB site in woodland on the Westwick Estate. 220 Infantry Brigade was based at Westwick House. The hide was accessed through a drop-down shaft and had an emergency exit passage constructed from a number of 40-gallon drums that had their tops and bottoms removed and were arranged so they would form a tunnel. The patrol's ammunition and explosives supplies were stored in the cellar of the farmhouse, much to the consternation of Cpl Tofts' mother.

The sites of Stody *(left)* and Alby Patrols' operational bases, both in disused sand/gravel pits

Ever since their abandonment in the mid-1940s, operational bases have made ideal homes for a number of wild animals including foxes, badgers, rabbits, toads, grass snakes and adders, bumble bees and wasps, not to mention the gazillions of fat black spiders. Although burrowing animals (especially rabbits) can cause considerable damage they also sometimes manage to expose telltale signs such as the top of the roofline of Aylsham Patrol's OB.

Alby Patrol's ammunition was located at a safe distance but within sight of the operational base. A small depression remains and it the corroded top of a 40-gallon drum can be seen *(in foreground)*. Considering that by no means all ammunition and explosives were collected after stand-down, sites such as this one are best left alone.

The north-west tower at Baconsthorpe Castle which conveniently accommodated the Anderson shelter used as Baconsthorpe Patrol's OB.

The currently waterlogged tower base at Baconsthorpe Castle *(left)* and the patrols' crawlspace which was dug at the bottom of the gap between the tower and the adjoining curtain wall *(right)*.

The upper roofline of Stody Patrol's OB. Part of the corrugated sheeting lining the earthen walls of the now collapsed entrance shaft is still in place.

Remains of what appears to be carpet underlay or felt, held in place by wire mesh, in situ on the partially collapsed rear wall (Stody).

Remains of the ammunition store of Matlaske Patrol

NORFOLK GROUP 4

In a letter dated 20 April 1943, GCO Lt Alfred George Douglas Greenshields of Neatishead informs his patrol leaders:

> "It has now been confirmed by HQ that I am to have the assistance of Lt Wm Eades of Frettenham, who is the eldest member of Aux Units excluding myself in the County, and Lt H Wharton of Mautby. The administration of the Group will remain as heretofore, except that either myself or one of the above mentioned Officers will be present at the firing of ammunition or the detonating of explosives. For the purpose of initial training, the responsibility of Mautby and South Walsham has been transferred to Lt Wharton and that of Hoveton and Neatishead to Lt Eades. This leaves Ludham and Happisburgh nominally under my control but as I have administrative work to deal with I shall call upon one or other of the above officers to assist me in the training of these two Sections."
> *(See Appendices E and F)*

Happisburgh Patrol: Sgt George Mervyn Deane; Cpl Hubert Barnard Sands; Pte William Love; Pte John Edward Owles (farmer); Pte Philip John Harmer (farmer); Pte Dr Alexander Herbert Dawson (veterinary doctor); Pte P Harmer (farmer); Pte George Milligan

Happisburgh Patrol's operational base was an elephant shelter with a drop-down shaft which was lined with corrugated sheets. The entrance opening was covered by a trap door. A pipe hidden in a hollow tree stump was reportedly used for dropping messages. A small room used for storing explosives adjoined the main chamber. The course of the unusually long emergency exit tunnel can still be seen. It followed a zigzag course measuring about 45 metres in length and emerged at the edge of the woodland. The whole length of this exit passage was covered with corrugated sheeting. After the war, the Forestry Commission removed the structure and a deep crater is all that remains. Army specialists trained the men in the use of explosives and sticky bombs and they attended training courses held near Aldershot in Hampshire and at Rackheath Hall.

Hoveton Patrol: Sgt LS Harris (school teacher), replaced by Sgt JR Howes (farmer); Cpl BC Durrant (estate worker); Pte Vic B Allen; Pte WS Collinge (farmer); Pte JG Nash; Pte CJ Colchester

The patrol's operational base was an elephant shelter located in the grounds of Hoveton Hall. It was accessed through a drop-down shaft, the earthen walls of which were lined with corrugated sheeting. The emergency passage was at the opposite end of the main chamber which has long since collapsed and become inaccessible. A few glazed ceramic ventilation pipes remain in situ.

Neatishead Patrol: Sgt Bertie William Charles Cox: Cpl Philip George Jolly; Pte Charles William Bush; Pte Harry Harvey; Pte Edward Albert Kirk; Pte Stanley Herbert Storey; Pte AW Blake

The operational base was an elephant shelter built in a private wood, not far distant from a quiet country lane. It had brick end walls and a deep, brick-built drop-down shaft. The OB has long since collapsed and only an overgrown depression in the ground remains.

Broken crockery found at the Hoveton OB site

a. G. D. Greenshield.

A. G. D. GREENSHIELDS.

Tel. No.: HORNING 206. HORNING 206.
STATION: WROXHAM.

WROXHAM

Hollygrove
Neatishead,
Norfolk.

HOLLYGROVE.

NEATISHEAD.

NORFOLK.

D. J. J. H
L. S. H.
E. M. H.
A. G. D. G.

SECRET

EXCERCISE 'FLORENCE'

GENERAL IDEA.

NORFOLK.

1. During May the Germans, having failed in their offensive in Russia assumed the defensive in the East, and began to transfer large forces to the West.
By June 2 it was clear that full preparations were being made for an early invasion of Great Britain. Britain BRITAIN

2. Stand by was ordered on June 2.
Complete Readiness on June 4.
Action Stations on June 6.

3. On night 6/7 June, heavy bombing commenced of aerodromes, particularly fighter, in Norfolk, and during 7/6 this was reinforced by attacks by Paratps on Both Coltishall G43 and Bircham Newton G25 groups of aerodromes.
On the Coltishall area, although the Paratps were duly mopped up, they managed to complete havoc done by bombing to an extent which put the aerodrome out of action.
The Bircham Newton aerodrome was also put out of action.

4. At dawn June 8 airbourne landings were made in Burnham Market G26. Wells Next the Sea G36. and Weybourne G56 areas, followed by heavey attacks on the garrisons holding these areas. The garrisons, hard pressed, retired, with the exceptions of pockets, holding out in the areas so yet unspecified.

Exercise "Florence", written in Capt Greenshield's hand.
(Source: Lieutenant LS Harris, private papers)

67

NORFOLK GROUP 5

Group Commander Lt Harry Wharton (farmer)
assisted by Lt GV Bowles

From 1914 to 1917 Harry Wharton served with 1/1st Norfolk Yeomanry in Britain, Gallipoli, Egypt and Palestine, and on the Western Front with 12th Battalion Norfolk Regiment from 1917 to 1919. After the war he farmed the family's farm in Mautby and from 1940 until stand down in 1945 he served with AU as Group Commander of Norfolk Group 5.

Mautby Patrol: Sgt GH Wain; Pte EJ Nichols; Pte Leslie J Tungate; Pte AJK Woltorton; Pte SC Locke

Unlike most other patrols who chose the bank or slope for the location of their operational base, the men from Mautby Patrol built theirs into the upper rim of a large disused marl pit, probably because marl pits are generally not located on ground as dry as sand and gravel pits. The pit is surrounded by a copse with fields on all sides. A farm track leads past. The OB was an elephant shelter which appears to have been set directly into the ground. Corrugated sheeting was used to form the end walls. The structure has collapsed to a degree that makes it difficult to assess how it might once have looked. It appears to have had a drop-down entrance shaft and there are traces of an emergency exit at the opposite end, but the structure is too far deteriorated to be certain.

In an interview taken in 1984, Lt Wharton explains that the operational bases were underground Nissen huts with a secret entrance and equipped with all the best ammunitions one could think of.

> "Hitler was supposed to land on the east coast and they sent a team down to teach us how to live with one another underground for 10 days. We were meant to stay underground for 10 days and then come out and hit them by cutting their communications and blowing up railway lines etc."

South Walsham Patrol: Sgt Edmund John Starkings (farmer); Cpl WJ "Billy" Gould (nurseryman); Pte Brian L Evans (shop assistant); Pte Leslie R Smith; Pte Gillie J Starkings (farmer); Pte Jack W White; George Herbert Edrich (auctioneer & estate agent)

Located in the grounds of what in the 1940s would have been South Walsham Hall, the patrol's operational base was an elephant shelter which was purportedly built into the remains of a disused ice hole. This is a very low-lying area that has always been prone to flooding. The ground is wet if not to say swampy, and adjoined in the north by South Walsham Broad - not very suitable conditions for the construction of underground structures that were meant to provide a safe and dry haven. At the "staggering" height of 19 feet above sea level, the old ice hole was probably built at one of the highest and driest locations in the area. And with the ice hole already in place and, more importantly, not flooded, the patrol had made an excellent, if somewhat unusual choice. The main chamber was accessed through a drop-down entrance shaft. Traces remain of an emergency exit passage oat the opposite end where evidence of the existence of an exit tunnel can still be seen. Sections of the end walls, held in place by railway sleepers, have since fallen off and the main chamber has silted up, considerably raising the floor level. The OB/ice hole is one of the sites featured in Fairhaven Water Gardens which are open to the public.

Catfield Patrol: Sgt George Henry Mixer; Cpl JL Chapman; Pte RG Chapman; Pte HF Edwards; Pte Reggie "Rat" Moore (an explosives expert); Pte Oswald George Tovell; Pte Harry PE Neave

The patrol, also referred to as Ludham Patrol, trained locally and held exercises at Ludham airfield and some of the auxiliers also received training at Coleshill.

Harry Neave owned a number of farms and houses in the area including High House, Heath Farm, Lessingham House and Bleak House (where he had his workshops). Neave owned about 2000 acres at Laurels Farm and used to make pontoons for the Army during the war. Some of his workshops were located right beside the Yarmouth & North Norfolk railway line and trains came in every day to take away the pontoons. Most of the patrol members worked for him at the time. Rodney Mixer, who used to live at Coltishall, was the works manager and when Neave died after the war, aged 46, Mixer set up his own business. The patrol's OB has yet to be located. It is believed to have been near Ludham aerodrome.

Oswald G Tovell's daughter remembers that her father was a good friend of the Chapmans and with Harry Neave, and that George Mixer was his boss.

David Bailey recalls:

> "My Grandfather – Oswald George Tovell (approx age in 1940: 26) – had the blue and red 202 badge and always told us he was in a special Home Guard unit. Having read Adrian Hoare's book about the Norfolk Home Guard I realised what he meant. I remember my grandfather telling me (and my mother confirms it) that they had a base close to Ludham aerodrome, it was disguised as a haystack and I was told that they had "stuff in there for weeks". My mother also remembers weapons being kept at home. My grandfather also told me about training with regulars somewhere away from Norfolk (his first trip out the county!)."

The following information comes from an interview conducted with Group Commander Capt Harry Wharton, recorded by Peter M Hart for the Imperial War Museum/London in 1984:

> "I was the local Home Guard commander until one day, suddenly, the command was taken away from me and given to my younger brother *(Charles)*, and I was sent to Coleshill, HQ of the Auxiliary Units. I used to go there for training with some of my own men. There were barracks where we lived in and there were coalmines, or some mines, all underground. We worked underground and we used to go through there in different ways and disguises. We were trained very carefully so that we learnt our job.
>
> I had a squad on my farm at Mautby and our hideouts were Nissen huts, built underground, with secret entries and filled with all the best ammunitions you can think of. No doubt about that. Hitler was supposed to land on the east coast. I had one squad at my farm, one at Catfield, one at South Walsham, and our Nissen huts were buried and the Navy sent a team down to teach us how to live with one another underground for 10 days, you know, you get fed up with one another, and they taught us how to deal with that. They sent another unit down to blow the holes and cover us up.

We had special officers attached, from the War Office I suppose, and everything was kept secret. Local people were not supposed to know anything. In fact, we had one fellow who said if we were in danger of being given away by anyone it was our duty to shoot him or her. We had magnets (for blowing up the railway line), all sorts of explosives, everything we wanted but nothing was used. I guess everything was buried and is still there. People did not really notice it when huts were being put in the ground. My one was done in a wood and so was the one in South Walsham, and in Catfield it was underground, underneath a tree they came up out of, a hollow tree. These places are still there, as are the explosives, as far as I know.

There were plenty of other squads besides mine. I only covered the Caister – Yarmouth area. There were thousands. When we used to go to Coleshill for training, there were about 500 there every weekend when it was our turn to go. I used to take five of my local lads. My quartermaster still lives at Caister, Gilly Bowles. He used to be the local publican during the war. Another one of my lads is Bob Tungate, he is an OBE. He works for my brother now as a foreman. We said which men we wanted for our squads. You see, I used to go to my brother *(the local HG commander)* and collared a good one or two of his. He didn't like it, I expect. We didn't take much part in the Home Guard; we might have paraded with them now and then. People perhaps wondered about what we were doing but we could not talk about it with anybody as we were sworn to secrecy."

Farmland between Catfield and Ludham - Catfield Patrol's OB is out there, somewhere

With its roof partially collapsed and the main chamber missing both end walls and silting up, the site of Mautby Patrol's Operational base is slowly reverting back to nature.

Glazed ceramic ventilation pipe exposed by burrowing rabbits (Hoveton OB).

The approximately 45 metres long zigzag course of the collapsed emergency exit passage, leading away from Happisburgh Patrol's OB site, can still clearly be seen.

Corrugated sheeting lines the rear wall of South Walsham Patrol's OB which was built into a disused ice hole situated in the grounds of South Walsham Hall

Collapsed entrance shaft at South Walsham Patrol's OB. The surrounding area has been landscaped and access into the main chamber has been blocked for health and safety reasons. Glazed ceramic ventilation pipes remain in situ, lodged in the topsoil above.

View of the partially collapsed roof of the main chamber of Mautby Patrol's OB

NORFOLK GROUP 6

GCO Lt Gerald Frederick Rutterford

Holkham Park Patrol: Sgt. EH Thompson; Cpl AJ Wroth; Pte RJC Green; Pte EA Wroth; Pte L Wroth; Pte WH Wroth; Pte GE Bix; Pte WA "Junior" Havers; Pte L Hewitt

Norfolk Group 6 is unique in that it appears to consist of only two patrols. It is difficult to perceive why Norfolk's northern coastline - an area extending over roughly 35 kilometres (22 miles), as the crow flies, from Hunstanton in the west to Cromer in the east - would have been covered by only one, very isolated patrol. The great number of coastal defence installations including the coast defence batteries at Hunstanton, Brancaster and Cromer, spigot mortar pedestals that can still be found in the dunes, and the countless pill boxes lined up along the cliff tops all attest to the fact that the coastline was considered to be vulnerable.

It is, however, true that the locations of AU patrols frequently concentrated in the vicinity of important transport routes, railway lines and aerodromes, and perhaps it was due to the lack of infrastructure, the scarcity of suitable locations, that accounts for the lack of patrols along the north coast. Perhaps it was simply a matter of not finding suitable men so that more patrols could have been set up. Perhaps more patrols did exist but were disbanded before stand-down, and patrol members' names were not recorded, for one reason or another. Perhaps a number of operational bases still await discovery. Only the future will tell.

Like many of their colleagues, the Holkham men favoured a disused sandpit as the location for their operational base. It was an elephant shelter located in a small wood on the Holkham Estate. Access was through a drop down shaft that was concealed under a hollow tree trunk. The end walls were built from red brick, with a central doorway in each. A toilet cubicle was incorporated in the emergency exit passage, which was covered by corrugated sheeting supported by timbers. A small storage area had been created near the end of the exit passage. The structure is partially collapsed and silted up.

Brancaster Patrol: Sgt Francis Edward Robinson; Sgt Bertie Cecil Griffin; Cpl Henry Robert "Harry" Payne; Pte John Thomas "Jack" Payne; Pte William Palmer; Pte David Lennie Raven; Pte William Robert Dix; and perhaps DJ Sparke

Five of the patrol members worked on Field House Farm under farm manager Lt Gerald Frederick Rutterford, the Group 6 GCO. The Patrol's OB has never been found. Considering that all patrol members worked on the farm, which stands isolated several kilometres to the south of the coastal village of Brancaster, it is plausible to conclude that the patrol might have used the farm (or a building on the farm) as their hideout as has already been documented from Ashill and Kirby Bedon Patrols, where all the patrol members were also working on the same farm.

From left: Sgt FE Robinson – farm worker; Sgt BC Griffin – gardener, handyman; Pte DL Raven; Lt GF Rutterford – farm manager; Pte Wm Palmer – gamekeeper; Pte Jack Payne or Cpl Harry Payne – brothers, both tractor drivers. All were employees of Field House Farm, Brancaster. *(Photo source unknown, BROM Archive)*

Lt Gerald Frederick Rutterford

He was the Commander of Norfolk Group 6 and worked as farm manager at Field House, a large farm near the village of Brancaster on the north Norfolk coast. *(Photo source unknown)*

NORFOLK GROUP 7

GCO Lt Richard Ralph "Dick" Stanton, Manor Farm, Dersingham, assisted by Sgt J Young and Sgt W Newstead

Dersingham Patrol: Sgt WG Cunningham; Sgt Fred J. Burton; Cpl W C Walden (carpenter); Pte Robert E Codman; Pte Walter H Cross; Pte J Futter; Pte E Parsons; Pte AF Doggett; Pte LH 'Paddy" Batterbee (thatcher); Pte Frank Goff (shepherd); Pte Richard R Griggs; Pte WHS Riches; Pte Clarence W Todd (gamekeeper) – all the men worked at Manor Farm, Dersingham.

The patrol is sometimes referred to as Sandringham Patrol, presumably because their operational base was situated on the Royal Sandringham Estate. Rumour has it that one of the rhododendron bushes in Sandringham Woods always flowers later than all others because it had been dug up and replanted after the OB had been built. According to another rumour there used to be an underground tunnel leading from the operational base to Sandringham House. Neither can be verified.

It is not known who it was that dug the hole for the patrol's operational base - the patrol members or their helpers, the Royal Engineers. The structure was an elephant shelter and its glazed ceramic ventilation pipes were hidden between tree roots. The structure was removed after the war and the remaining hole partially filled in. Traces of the collapsed emergency escape tunnel can still be seen. With the King's Lynn to Hunstanton railway line and Sandringham House nearby the patrol would have concentrated on training as to how best to blow up railways lines. They regularly attended courses held at Leicester Square Farm.

Ringstead Patrol: Sgt WG Cunningham; Cpl WC Walden; Pte RE Codman; Pte WH Cross; Pte J Futter; Pte E Parsons; Pte Arthur F Doggett

Ringstead patrol, sometimes also referred to as Heacham Patrol – presumably because of the close proximity of their OB's location to the village of Heacham - was dug into a thick layer of chalk deposited here during the ice age, in a copse situated on the edge of Ringstead Downs Nature Reserve. The structure has since been removed or collapsed. Judging from the remains, it was built from corrugated sheeting, red-brick, angle iron and wood. Four weathered and overgrown wooden corner posts appear to be still in their original position.

Snettisham Patrol: Sgt George Rex Carter; Sgt WA Whitby (discharged); Pte John B Betts (estate/farm manager;) Pte Walter E Claxton; Pte A "Harry" C Hazle; Pte David W Jarvis (farm worker); Pte Gordon R Winner; Pte Derek V Smith

The patrol's OB was located in a private wood in the grounds of Ken Hill Estate. It consisted of an elephant shelter, which was accessed through a not very deep drop-down shaft. The main chamber contained four wooden bunks that were arranged along its sides. Candles were apparently used for lighting and the soot-blackened tin (possibly Army issue) candleholders were left behind when the dugout was abandoned after stand-down. *(Source: unverified eye witness account)*. The structure was removed in the 1960s after it had partially collapsed. Traces of the escape tunnel can still be seen and a glazed ceramic ventilation pipe remains in situ.

Patrol leader Sgt Carter was a local man employed by Etna Stone & Shingle Co, Snettisham, who manufactured many items that were used in the construction of RAF camps during the war, and for some time he worked for the estate and later as a lorry driver. John Betts was the estate's farm manager. The men trained locally as well as at Leicester Square Farm. In the event of an invasion their targets would have been the RAF Combined Gunnery Range at Snettisham as well as several aerodromes in the vicinity and the LNER (King's Lynn to Hunstanton) railway line.

The site of Snettisham Patrol's OB in a privately owned wood on Ken Hill Estate.

Sgt George Rex Carter (2nd row centre), leader of Snettisham Patrol.
(Photo source: Susan Garwell)

Site of Ringstead Patrol's OB near the edge of a copse by Ringstead Downs Nature Reserve.
Farm rubbish has been dumped in the depression. Wooden corner posts remain in situ.

View of the rear brick-built wall with emergency exit opening *(left)* and brick-built entrance shaft at Holkham Park Patrol's OB.

A deep depression marks the site of the removed elephant shelter at Dersingham Patrol's OB. The course of the emergency exit tunnel *(right)* can still be seen.

Picture of Auxiliary Units patrol members from Group 8 taken in 1943
(Photo source: Desmond Neville)

Back row left to right:

Aubrey Brown (Mintlyn Patrol), EW Causton (Gayton Patrol), Jack Masters (Castle Rising Patrol), unknown, Dick Libbey (Mintlyn Patrol), Edwin Seaman (Mintlyn Patrol), Ray Mallett (Narford Patrol), Ron Bennett (Narford Patrol), Rex Robin (Middleton Patrol), Bob Eggleton (Gayton Patrol), Deryck Neville (Castle Rising, later transferred to Middleton Patrol), GR Grief (Gayton Patrol)

Middle row:

Stanley Warren (Castle Rising Patrol), Sgt Walter Garner (Castle Rising Patrol), Sgt Harold Spreckley (Mintlyn Patrol), Capt EJ Robinson (promoted from Castle Rising Patrol to A & Q Group 11 Norfolk AU, Capt JL Hardy (GCO), Lt Maurice Newnes (assist. GCO), Sgt H Haggas (Gayton Patrol), Sgt GF Attwood (Narford Patrol), Cpl Cheddar Walker (Mintlyn Patrol), Cpl D Sneezum (Narford Patrol)

Front row:

Archie Hudson (Castle Rising Patrol), unknown, Ernie Drew (Castle Rising Patrol), RW Pennell (Gayton Patrol), Bill Ely (Mintlyn Patrol), Ted Welham (Gayton Patrol), Sgt H Shackcloth (Gayton Patrol), Ted Masters (Castle Rising Patrol)

NORFOLK GROUP 8

GCO Capt Jocelyn Leslie Hardy DSO MC, King's Lynn,
assisted by Lt. Maurice Newnes, a solicitor from King's Lynn

Built by the men themselves, most of the operational bases in this group are either collapsed or they were destroyed or removed after the war, leaving hardly a trace. The OB used by the men from Ashill Patrol is presumed to be in good condition but alas, it has long since been made inaccessible.

Castle Rising Patrol: Sgt Thomas Walter Garner (farmer); Sgt Leonard Stanley Chester Warren (auctioneer's clerk); Sgt EJ Robinson (transferred and promoted to Capt, Admin Quartermaster); Pte Ernest Victor Drew (farm worker); Pte Archie Hudson (farm worker); Pte Arthur Edward Masters (farm worker); Pte John Robert Christopher William Masters (farm worker); Pte Chester Fordham Robin (salesman); Pte Deryck GH Neville (transferred to Middleton Patrol in March 1943)

Most of the men in Castle Rising Patrol worked on patrol leader Sgt Walter Garner's farm. They built their OB on the edge of a copse located on the farm's land but it soon became apparent that the hideout was uninhabitable. During an exercise where they were meant to spend the weekend in their OB to acclimatise themselves the candles went out repeatedly due to lack of oxygen, and after one of the patrol members almost passed out for lack of air the hide was abandoned. A second operational base was built several miles away in the Black Hill area. It has long since collapsed and a shallow depression is all that remains.

Ashill Patrol: Sgt John Kenneth Broadhead (farmer); Sgt Stanley William Burroughs; Pte Reginald Herbert Clutterham (farm worker); Pte David John Fake; Pte George Dewing; Pte W Sanderson (farmer); Pte Samuel Edward Mortimer

The patrol was disbanded before stand-down and all the members were returned to their local Home Guard unit. Fortunately their names were recorded whilst the patrol was still operational.

Uncharacteristically the operational base used by Ashill Patrol was not built in a sandpit or in woods away from human habitation but - similar to Kirby Bedon (Norfolk Group 2) patrol's OB - underneath the floor of a farm shed at Burys Hall. At the time Burys Hall was owned by patrol leader Sgt JK Broadhead's family. The 250th Special Tunnelling Coy built the operational base. It had a trap door entrance and an escape hatch in the adjoining cart shed. A number of bunks were fitted on each side of the chamber and the patrol's explosives were stored underneath these bunks as well as on shelves. The OB had electric lighting, a toilet and an Army field telephone. Ventilation was provided via a drainpipe on the side of the building. Army specialists trained the patrol members and they attended courses at Leicester Square Farm. They all had revolvers and they shared a Thompson submachine gun and a Sten gun. The patrol used a hollow tree opposite the farm as their observation post. It was accessed through a trapdoor in the bottom. Ancient oaks still line the road leading past Bury's Hall.

Patrol member Reginald Clutterham recalls:

> "I was a farm worker which was a reserved occupation. When they appealed for Local Defence Volunteers I joined up, I was 27 at the time. I was not in the LDV/Home Guard for long before, one day, a man came to interview me at my boss, Mr Broadhead's house at Burys Hall. I was asked if I would like to do something more interesting than the Home Guard and told that if I wanted to join this special organisation I would have to sign the Official Secrets Act... My wife knew nothing about my activities in the Auxiliary Units, I told my family I was in the Home Guard and wore that uniform."

Patrol member David John Fake remembers:

> "On one exercise at an aerodrome someone challenged us and said 'what are you doing here? This is a Free French aerodrome. We shoot first and ask questions later.' It was the only Free French aerodrome in Norfolk and apparently we should not have been on it." *(NB: It appears that DJ Fake was mistaken, as there never appears to have been a Free French aerodrome in Norfolk).*

Gayton patrol: Sgt Herbert "Bertie" James Haggas; Pte EW Causton; Pte RW Eggle(s)ton; Pte GR Grief; Pte RW Pennell; Pte HE Shackcloth; Pte FP Welham

Gayton patrol's operational base shares its fate with all but one in this group. Located near the edge of a privately owned wood, it had a drop-down entrance shaft and the main chamber was an elephant shelter. The structure was removed after the war and a much overgrown rectangular depression filled with tree stumps and branches is all that remains.

Middleton Patrol: Sgt Alfred George Sykes (farmer); Sgt Ralph Burman (left in 1941); Pte William Thomas Bedford (farmer); Pte Daniel S Crawford; Pte Johnny Narborough (worked for ICI); Pte G F "Fuzzy" Howes; Pte Deryck GH Neville (transferred from Castle Rising patrol in March 1943); Pte Arthur Robert Wilson (farmer)

The patrol's operational base was built in sandy soil in a small privately owned wood between the North West Norfolk villages of Middleton and East Winch. It had a drop-down entrance shaft, the cover of which could be unlocked with a key that was kept hidden on the base of a nearby pine tree. The trap door was covered with roofing felt. The men built their OB themselves, using corrugated sheeting that rested on railway sleepers for constructing the roof. The walls of the main chamber, which had a recess for storing explosives and a toilet cubicle, were lined with roadside kerbstones. All the building materials were "borrowed" from local sources. An escape tunnel was added later. The patrol also had an emergency bolthole in a copse on nearby Ferret's Hill. The men targeted the railway lines in the area as well as the nearby aerodromes at West Raynham and Marham.

Mintlyn patrol: Sgt Harold Charles Spreckley (chemist); Cpl Fredrick William Walker; Pte Ernest William Baker: Pte William James Ely; Pte Aubrey *(Erk?)* Brown; Pte Richard Pearse Libbey; Pte Edwin De Gray Seaman

A shallow depression in the ground marks the location where Mintlyn Patrol's OB once was, not far from a disused railway line near a large gravel extraction site not far south from the B1145 road. The main chamber was removed after the war but a short gully denoting the course of the emergency exit passage can still be seen. The emergency exit was discovered by chance about 40 years, when the peg of a snare (for catching rabbits) would not go into the ground. Further investigation brought to light a steel trapdoor, covered by a layer of soil and leaf mould. The rhododendron bush growing beside it is still flourishing.

Narford Patrol: Sgt George Frederick Attwood (estate manager); Cpl Dennis Sneezum; Pte Ralph Ronald "Ron" Bennett; Pte Robert Joseph Mallett (farmer); Pte William Welham (gamekeeper); Pte GW Howard

Despite extensive searches conducted in the area, Narford Patrol's operational base has so far eluded discovery. It is believed to be situated in the grounds of Narford Hall. One of the patrol members, since diseased, has described it as collapsed, more than a decade ago, and another has described the site as being situated near the 7th tree, without elaborating on the location where this tree might be found.

The rhododendron bush marks the spot where the trap door of Mintlyn Patrol's OB used to be.

Ashill Patrol's OB was located beneath the floor of the white-washed corner building, which had to be entered in order to get to the trap door in the floor.

The site of Castle Rising Patrol's second operational base at Black Hills.

The men from Castle Rising Patrol, from left to right: Ernie Drew, Rex Robin, Stanley Warren, Jack Masters, Deryck Neville, Ted Masters and Archie Hudson, with Sgt JW Walter Garner sitting in the chair in front of the group. Deryck Neville had already transferred to Middleton Patrol but was invited to join his colleagues for the occasion. *(Photo source: Desmond Neville)*

A deep (and very much overgrown) depression marks the site of Gayton Patrol's OB. The elephant shelter was removed after the war.

GCO Capt WW Ward,
assisted by Lt James Woods and Lt Longfields

Both the operational bases of the two patrols in this group are located in the grounds of the Somerleyton Estate, which includes Fritton Lake, where extensive and very secret experiments involving the testing of duplex drive amphibious tanks were conducted during the war. The whole area was surrounded by electric fences and armed guards manned the entrances. Tenants of the estate cottages had to go through gated areas with a guard stationed there to let them in and out and they had to sign the Official Secrets Act. The first units arrived at Fritton Lake by train in April 1943, to begin the secret technical trials. About 150 troops were stationed at Fritton Lake permanently and a squadron or unit at a time, in total, about 1,000 people were trained there. Troops from regiments across the country were sent, as well as soldiers from Canada and America. The converted floating Valentine and Sherman tanks were developed for the D-Day landings when they were intended to come to shore with the first wave of infantry, to provide heavy artillery support and then take out all the defences.

Waveney Forest, a wood across the road, was the site of a WW2 military training camp which, at times, was linked to the activities at Fritton Lake. The history of Waveney Forest as the location of various military activities, however, reaches back to the times of the Great War. Consequently, the wood is traversed by trenches and pockmarked by a great number of crater-like depressions. It also houses altogether 20 small underground structures (at two separate locations), with concrete roofs and earthen walls that were stabilised by what appears to be Hessian sacking and wire mesh in timber frames – too small to be OBs even if they stood on their own rather than aligned in rows, one next to the other. One of the many craters in Waveney Forest is considerably deeper and also much larger than all others. It is located in what at the time would have been a fairly secluded area. Galvanised netting and angle-iron posts are still in situ, and a length of cast iron pipe is lying on its upper rim. It is possible that this crater was caused by blowing up an operational base, perhaps the first OB of one of the two patrols operating in the area. They certainly would have had to abandon their hideout when the military occupied the area in 1942, or risk being arrested or shot.

Fritton Patrol: Sgt Hugh Mowbray Salmon – replaced by Sgt George Henry Blyth; Pte Wilfred Harold Meadows; Pte Henry Frederick Watson; Pte John Charles White; Pte Sydney George Howlett; Pte William "Bill" Leech (transferred); Pte WR Grint; Pte John "Jack" Charles Reeman (transferred); PJ Gee (transferred)

George Henry Blyth's grandson, Simon, recalls:

> "My grandfather left Church Road school at the age of 14 and went to work on a cattle farm near Lound and Ashby. It was here where he learnt to ride horses bareback. He delivered milk from the farm until the war broke out. He got married in 1938 and moved to Fritton in 1939. Because of a heart murmur, caused by rheumatic fever when he was eight years old, he couldn't be enlisted in the Army. He worked as a milk deliveryman for Longs Humberstone diary, which was the main centre for milk distribution in the area and joined the Home Guard, when his name was anonymously put forward for Auxiliary Units. He was accepted to the secret training course (at Coleshill House) and told us later how they were taught to kill using a knife, how to use explosives and how to build booby

traps. Granddad was promoted to sergeant and soon became an expert in explosives. They used to blow up trees to practise. He was issued a sniper rifle, revolver, grenades and a commando knife.

Many years later granddad still said very little about Auxiliary Units, though he did describe how a load of manual workers were brought down to Fritton and elsewhere from "up north" to set up underground dens with secret escape tunnels, without knowing where they were. These were situated near hollow trees to allow piping of smoke at tree top level to reduce the risk of detection, thus providing them with warmth and the ability to cook.

Dad can recall playing with bullets and pistol (but not together) that were stored in a box under the stairs (until 1946). Detonators were also kept in the house. Only in the 1970s, when the gamekeeper discovered their dugout, did he speak about it. But he was never clear about the site. Dad thinks it was somewhere near the end of Blocka Run."

The patrol was sometimes also referred to as St Olaves or Herringfleet Patrol. Their operational base was located within walking distance of the OB of the only other patrol in this group, lead by private Bill Leech's brother, Russell Leech, and within a stone's throw of a cottage which at the time was occupied by WR Grint, one of the patrol members. Twenty-five-year old photographs show that the main chamber was an elephant shelter. The emergency exit tunnel had perhaps already collapsed by the time the pictures were taken, provided there was one, because no trace of it can be discerned in the photographs.

The whole structure has since collapsed and its remains are contained within a roughly rectangular depression. Access was through a drop-down shaft and then through a passage built from red brick, the lower part of which had a number of steps leading down into the main chamber. The main chamber's brick end walls are still in place, albeit quite overgrown, and a length of wooden board with some nails, affixed to the wall beside the entrance doorway and presumably used for hanging up coats, is also still in situ.

Remains of what appears to have been a smaller room adjoining the far wall indicate that the patrol might have used a second, smaller chamber either for storage or for keeping their explosives. The men used a homemade, fairly large, square section of corrugated sheeting, bent into a square shape, to serve as their ventilation pipe.

Private William "Bill" Leech, who used to drive to the operational base on his motorcycle, left the patrol in 1943 to serve with No. 6 Commando. He travelled to Coleshill House for training and used to practice stealth at the Brooke Marine shipyard at night, successfully dodging the night watchman.

Private Jack Reeman joined the patrol when he was 18 (the patrol was already established by then) and he remained with the group for 2 years before being called up to join the Royal Navy.

Fritton Lake Patrol: Sgt Russel Robert Leech (builder, brother of Pte Bill Leech in Fritton Patrol); Pte Sydney Clement Arthur "Stan" Fuller (shop worker); Pte Wm John Thomas Dolder (farmer); Pte Donald Thomas Colebrook (electrician at Brook Marina); Pte Brian G Rudd; Pte Sydney Porter; Pte RJ Botwright (hairdresser); Pte F Fletcher (boat builder); Pte Arthur G Gooch (electrician)

The patrol was also referred to as Somerleyton Patrol. It is not known who built the patrol's OB, which was a large elephant shelter consisting of two chambers which were accessed through a drop-down shaft that was 3.50 metres (11+ feet) deep. The curved roof is resting on concrete plinths that were painted off-white. The entrance opening was secured by a cover which could be moved by pulling a wire attached to a heavy, pivoted concrete counterweight, still in situ at the bottom of the shaft, where it landed after the chain it was attached to had corroded.

The shaft's earthen walls were lined with corrugated sheeting. Corrugated sheeting also formed the end walls of both chambers, one of which has since collapsed, as has the adjoining emergency exit passage. A number of glazed ceramic drain pipes provided sufficient ventilation.

The floor level at the far end of the main chamber has been raised to form a platform which is level with the top of the plinths on both sides. The main chamber contained four sleeping platforms which are still in situ, placed on their sides and resting against the curved wall. They are 2.50 metres (8+ feet) long and were constructed from pine bearers with roughly cut slats laid across. One side of the slats is covered with what appears to be roofing felt, presumably to protect the sleeping men from rising dampness. The platforms would have been laid across the width of the chamber, resting on the plinths when in use. There is no trace of the chimney that the operational base is said to once have had. This could have been in the second chamber which has collapsed.

Patrol member Billy Leech (Fritton Patrol) photographed on the occasion of a visit to his operational base in the 1980s when the main chamber was still intact. *(Photo: Jack Grice)*

The collapsed main chamber of Fritton Patrol's OB in 2012.

Rear wall of the main chamber of Fritton Lake OB. The adjoining second chamber has collapsed.

Corrugated sheeting held in place by a sturdy timber frame *(left)* and the concrete trapdoor counterweight - note the pivots, made from a section of gas pipe. The counterweight is covered with a layer of tar. (Fritton Lake OB)

Sleeping platforms in Fritton Lake OB. The black material adhering to the wooden slats appears to be roofing felt.

GCO Capt Walter G Gentle,
assisted by Lt Eric G Field, Lt RF St B Wayne, Lt DC Carey and Sgt GR Holmes

Lt DC Carey farmed at Walsingham. Interestingly, he appears in the list of Walsingham Patrol as their patrol leader - he certainly seems to have been a busy man.

Capt Walter G Gentle lived in Brandon where he was a local butcher and pig farmer, specialising in breeding saddleback pigs. The (secret) nickname given to him by members of the patrols he was in charge of was "Hoggie". In 1945, Capt Gentle was awarded the M.B.E "for services rendered to the 202 (GHQ) Reserve Battalion, Home Guard during the last four years". He had already been awarded the Military Cross in the First World War.

Norfolk Group 10 consisted of three patrols which operated in the South Norfolk - North Suffolk border area between Brandon and Lakenheath and of two scattered patrols, one near Fakenham and the other near East Dereham, roughly, 20 miles (30 kilometres) distant, as the crow flies. Two of the four men assisting GCO Capt Gentle were from the Fakenham/East Dereham area though, and hence in a position to look after the two more distant patrols.

Brandon Patrol: Sgt Philip R. Field (brother of Lt Eric Field, assist GCO); Cpl S. William "Bill" Baker; Pte Roy D. Budden (garage owner from Elveden); Pte Albert L. Drewry; Pte George A. Eagle; Pte George H. Holden; Pte D Smith; Pte J William "Billy" Stead; Pte Walter Blake (farmer)

The small town of Brandon is located in the Breckland area on the border of Suffolk with the adjoining county of Norfolk but like some other Suffolk patrols in the Norfolk – Suffolk border region it is listed under Norfolk Auxiliary Units patrols. In all likelihood Brandon was chosen as one of the bases for an Auxiliary Units patrol because it was thought that an invading German Army might rest up and regroup in the cover of the extensive woodlands of Thetford Forest. There was also a need to control the strategic road junction between East Anglia and the Midlands, along with Brandon's excellent rail links and the large flat expanses of Breckland heathland which, without a doubt, would have made an ideal landing area for parachutists. The 46th Division was based at nearby Didlington Hall.

The patrol's first operational base was built in Forestry Plantation. It is said to have provided sufficient space for 15 men. The base, however, was prone to flooding and had to be abandoned.

A second OB was constructed on the edge of Lingheath, an area of scrubby woodland adjoining Thetford Forest. After clearing brush from the ground the trapdoor could be opened. The main chamber had a flat roof constructed from corrugated sheeting resting on sections of tree trunks, and it contained eight bunks and a Primus stove. The OB has since either collapsed or was removed and no trace remains. The patrol's observation post was located near Bury Road.

The patrol members were equipped with a dozen Mills bombs, High Explosive plastic, 20-minute time pencil fuses, detonators and five and ten-minute fuse wire (for railway sabotage). They trained locally and met every Saturday in the nearby chalk pit on the Elveden to Bury St Edmunds road. They men were taught by regular Army how to prime and throw Mills bombs, how to dismantle fuses and how to wrap plastic explosive around rail tracks to cut 3-foot lengths of rail. At another joint-training day the participants were instructed in tank sabotage, how to keep a low profile and how to use their revolvers. The unit sometimes also used to travel to North Norfolk where they trained on the rifle range at Cawston heath.

East Dereham Patrol: Sgt Hugh Edward Parfitt; Cpl Matthew Harvey Thompson; Pte Redvers Cyril Beck; Pte John Goram; Pte Fredrick Henry Ottoway; Pte Ernest William Pratt; Pte Bernard Percival Walpole; Pte A C Wright (discharged); Pte M M Wilson; Pte/Cpl Phillip George Jolly

No information has at the time of going to press come to light concerning East Dereham Patrol and the activities of its members. The location of the patrol's operational base has as yet to be discovered. It is believed to be located in a private wood near North Elmham.

Fakenham Patrol: Sgt Bertam Warnes; Cpl Charles John Williams; Pte George Brown; Pte Ralph Fuller; Pte Harry Gates; Pte Donald Frank Gilder; Pte Ernest "Ernie" Charles Huggins (blacksmith); Pte F J Napp; Pte G Dawson

Fakenham Patrol's operational base is located on the Fakenham side of the Raynham Estate. It was an elephant shelter, built into deposits of alluvial sands and gravels with its elevated location offering panoramic views. The entrance shaft collapsed several decades ago, when forestry workers clearing up after the Great Storm in 1967 accidentally drove heavy machinery over it. No trace remains of the emergency exit passage. The main chamber is intact, with sections of corrugated sheeting lining the end walls still in situ, as is one of the glazed ceramic ventilation pipes. An observation post may have been situated nearby.

Hockwold Patrol: Sgt Walter T Cooper; Cpl A Maggs; Pte Ronald Bartlett; Pte Jessie Alfred Morley Enefer; Ernest AA Hicks; Ray C Rolph; AE Starking

Hockwold Patrol's operational base was located in wood near Feltwell Lodge. It was an elephant shelter with an adjoining ammunition store, and a long escape run leading into the woods. Over the years, part of the area has been transformed into a quarry and it is currently used as a landfill site. No trace remains of the operational base.

Lakenheath Patrol: Sgt Fred Arthur Crowther (farmer); Cpl Hector Wm Crocker; Pte George Palfrey (farmer); Pte Alva (?) Ernest Rolph; Pte Sidney Wm Rolph; Pte Horace Wm Smith; Pte Reginald Henry Thomas Young; Pte RP Meen

The patrol was sometimes also referred to as Thetford Patrol. No information is currently available as to the patrol members' activities or the whereabouts of their operational base.

View across the landfill site near Feltwell Lodge - no trace remains of Hockwold Patrol's operational base, which was situated in this area.

The men from Brandon Patrol *(Photo source: JR Field)*
Back row L to R: Billy Stead – Group CO Walter Gentle – Wally Blake
Middle row L to R: Sgt Philip Field – assist CO Eric Field *(holding the cup)* - Roy D. Budden
Front row L to R: George A. Eagle - Cpl. S. William "Bill" Baker

The site of Brandon Patrol's operational base on Lingheath.

Fakenham Patrol's OB has lost sections of its end walls and is silted up but the main chamber is intact. A circular opening in the corrugated sheeting that formed part of the end wall *(left)* marks the spot where a ventilation pipe would once have been passed through.

GCO Lt LN Brock,
assisted by Sgt JE Taylor

Alethorpe (Ailthorpe) Patrol: Sgt Guy Savory (farmer); Cpl John Cedric Thistleton-Smith (farmer); Pte Alec Newstead (farm worker); Pte Charles Cornwall; Pte John D Burgess (farmer); Pte Alec Savory (brother of Guy – he was 10 years older than Guy, served in WWI and spent 18 months as a POW)

Corporal JC Thistleton-Smith was a member of the Norfolk Cricket Team, taking part in Minor Counties Championships from 1930 to 1951. He also owned Alethorpe Hall, in the grounds of which the patrol's operational base was built.

The operational base is an elephant shelter, dug into level ground near the edge of a copse. A farm track leads past the wood's edge. The main chamber, which had a drop-down entrance shaft at one end and an emergency exit passage at the other, is missing one end wall but otherwise intact. The end walls were constructed from corrugated sheeting held in place by a wooden frame. The interior walls were painted off-white. Four 40-gallon drums aligned lengthwise, two on each side of the exit doorway, held the patrol's water supply. Also still in situ is a glazed ceramic ventilation pipe and a wooden strainer post with a long nail sticking out of its end, near where the exit passage would have emerged on ground level.

Regular soldiers at Leicester Square Farm trained the patrol. The men also attended pistol training at Walsingham.

Blakeney Patrol: Sgt Hugh T Harcourt (farmer); Pte Peter Harcourt (son of HT Harcourt, recruited when 16 – part-time member); Pte George Cubitt; Pte John Edwin Betts; Pte Ernie Parsons; Pte Stanley J Taylor (discharged); Pte Albert R Holman; Pte Alan C Hudson, Oakdene, Blakeney (part-time member)

The patrol members went to Coleshill House for training and they also attended a 2-week course held at Leicester Square Farm and a 3-week course at Sandown on the Isle of Wight. Several Sunday mornings were spent at Lodge Hill, Sheringham. The men were equipped with .303 Enfield rifles, they had striker boards sewn to one trouser leg, daggers which were worn down the other leg and Smith & Wesson .38 revolvers. The patrol's OB was of Anderson shelter-type construction and located in a small wood on the southern edge of Wiveton Downs. The wood has since been cut down and the land transformed into arable. The chamber was pulled out of the ground and the corrugated sheeting was used for the construction of a few pig huts. No trace remains on the ground.

Cley Patrol: Sgt Jack A Barnard; Sgt Nicky Newstead; Cpl William R Bishop; Pte WJ Fuller; Pte Harry AW Hart; Pte Brian P Ramm (farmer); Pte Ronald Hill; Pte RA Lee; Pte C.E.P Allen

Cley Patrol members enjoyed fine views across the marshes and out to the North Sea from the location of their operational base. It was built on the upper edge of a disused pit – one of many sand, gravel, chalk and marl pits all adjoining each other, in a hilly area known as "The Hangs". There are no accounts detailing the size and building materials, and the structure has sadly long since collapsed. Corrugated sheeting, length of timbers and steel girders remain at the entrance.

Thursford Patrol: Sgt A Scargill; Cpl Bernard H Flint; Pte CAF "Anthony" Bailey (farm manager); Pte Edward WC Davies (carpenter); Pte HC Lewis; Pte Alfred Smith; Pte T Brock

The patrol's first operational base appears to have been built by Army regulars. It soon turned out to be uninhabitable, though, and finally it had to be abandoned because of flooding. The men from Thursford Patrol chose an unusual location for their second OB. Contrary to almost all locations where operational bases were most commonly built - away from human habitation - theirs was situated right up to the high boundary wall on the edge of a small pasture that is adjoined by several cottages. The entrance to their hideout was cleverly concealed in one of the small outbuildings and sheds dotted in this pasture. This particular shed housed an outdoor toilet, which had to be accessed in order to reach the OB's entrance, a well-concealed trapdoor in the privy's sidewall. The main chamber was an elephant shelter that shared one of its red-brick walls with the adjoining privy, thanks to the close proximity of which the patrol members had no need for the installation of the usual Elsan toilet. A chimney pipe can still be seen emerging from the roof on the grassed over mound above, and glazed ceramic ventilation pipes are also still in situ. No traces remain of an emergency exit passage, if ever there was one.

Patrol member Anthony Bailey recalls:

> "Our first OB was built in Thursford wood by men from the regular Army although they did not know what it was for. Because it was near a spring it got flooded, so we had to dig our own hideout nearer to Thursford village."

The location of the first hideout is about 650 metres distant from the second OB site and lies 170 feet ASL, that is about 100 feet lower than its replacement. As a 4-year old boy, local resident Tom Cushing watched with his older brother from their home as a group of about 20 regular Army soldiers crossed one of their cornfields in single file, heading towards Thursford Wood. Curious, the two boys followed the soldiers' trail some time later and they came upon a small square dugout that was slowly filling up with water. They revisited the wood at a later time and found a new dugout about 20 metres distant from the first.

The OB was of a flat-topped design with earthen walls that were presumably stabilised with corrugated sheeting of which a small piece was found on the site. The depression is a good metre deep and measures 6.50 x 3.30 metres (20 x 10 feet) approximately. The OB's roof has collapsed more than two decades ago. The entrance shaft appears to have been at one corner. The 7 metres (24 feet) long, doglegged emergency escape exit led out the opposite end, further into the wood and away from the road, terminating beneath a rhododendron bush. Four sections of glazed ceramic vent pipes remain roughly in situ and one of the roof beams is also still in place, although very much deteriorated. The waterlogged smaller dugout found by the two boys only about 20 metres distant was probably intended to be used as an ammo store. No trace of it remains.

Walsingham Patrol: Lt DC Carey (farmer) - Lt Carey was also assistant GCO in Group 10. Most of the men in the patrol worked on his farm at Westgate. Sgt RL Wells; Cpl EW Beckham; Pte Dennis G Seaman; Pte George Able; Pte Sid Beckham, Pte GM Fray

Walsingham Patrol's OB was built in sandy soil near the edge of a privately owned wood on the Walsingham Estate, not far from a farm track. The main chamber was an elephant shelter with its end walls constructed from corrugated sheeting, held in place by a timber frame. The drop-down entrance shaft – accessed by a steel ladder - has collapsed, as has the emergency exit passage at the opposite end.

The chamber is intact but silted up, and the end wall near the collapsed entrance shaft is missing. A glazed ceramic ventilation pipe is still in situ as are three springers that would have been used for holding a shelf. The interior walls of the chamber were painted off-white.

A hollow tree trunk about 15 metres (16 yards) distant served as the patrol's observation post. It was purportedly accessed through a foxhole. A second observation post is said to have been located in an adjoining wood.

Exposed end wall and entrance doorway of Alethorpe Patrol's operational base the top of which is well covered with ivy.

The men from Alethorpe Patrol stored their water supply in these 40-gallon drums that were kept just inside the entrance to the operational base.

The site of Blakeney Patrol's operational base was in the far corner of the field seen on the right which in the 1940s was a small wood.

View from Cley Patrol's OB

The outdoor toilet within which the trapdoor giving access to Thursford Patrol's OB was concealed.

Corrugated sheeting forming the end walls of Walsingham Patrol's OB. The entrance shaft in front of it has collapsed, exposing the end wall and entrance doorway.

Springers for holding a shelf, in situ, in Walsingham Patrol's OB.

Norfolk Auxiliary Units Scout Sections

The civilians forming the AU operational patrols were supported and frequently also trained by members of AU Scout Sections. By November 1940 the regions covered by Auxiliary Units patrols had been divided into 14 areas, each commanded by an IO of their own. With the exception of Wales, each one of these areas was now assigned two Scout Sections, drawn from the county regiments and consisting of an officer and 11 other ranks plus transport. Together with the Scout Sections and the staff of the IOs' headquarters, the regular staff by now numbered more than 400.

After three months of initial training by their IO, the Scout Sections were in turn to train all the patrols operating in their region by giving lectures and demonstrations. They were also to organise night exercises. A good deal of their time was spent with constructing their own two operational bases as they would be split into two patrols of normal strength for operational purposes. By the time they had built these they were often considered by the IO as his working parties and asked to dig for those of the Home Guard who firmly declined to do so for themselves.

The East Norfolk Scout Section was based at Beech House, Wroxham, in the Norfolk Broads area - a spacious property situated down a quiet road on the outskirts of the Norfolk Broads village of Wroxham. The area was covered by several AU patrols – Mautby, South Walsham, Ludham, Neatishead and Hoveton - under GCOs Lt Harry Wharton of Mautby and Lt ADG Greenshields of Neatishead.

The west Norfolk Scout Section was based at Leicester Square Farm, and later near the village of Anmer. When in late 1942 – early 1943 the threat of an invasion had receded and some of the members of the section were called up or joined other organisations such as SAS, SOE, the Jedburghs *(a Special Forces unit)* or the Phantoms *(GHQ Liaison Regiment)*. The remaining men were amalgamated with the equally depleted West Norfolk Scout Section.

East Norfolk Scout Section

The Section comprised a dozen men including a lance corporal from Great Yarmouth, "Nobby" Clarke; in addition, there were a clerk, and Norfolk IO Capt George Woodward's driver. It is known that all men came from the 2nd and 7th Battalions of the Norfolk Regiment but only a handful of members' names, including their history, can be established.

> Lt Peter "Percy" Pike - son of a local garage owner
> Sgt (name unknown)
> Cpl Leslie Long - a hairdresser from London
> L/Cpl "Nobby" Clarke
> Recruit Victor Owen "Chalky" White, London
> Recruit Alfie Barffe
> Recruit Sid Mace
> Recruit Bob Butcher
> Recruit Thomas "Tom" Herbert Colquitt, Widnes, Cheshire

Beech House, home of the East Norfolk Scout Section and Norfolk Auxiliary Units HQ

The Wroxham property was a large private house, which formed part of the Trafford Estate. Some of the upstairs rooms were fitted with two to four military bunks. Lt Pike had his own room; the other members shared the remaining bedrooms. A non-operational clerk manned the downstairs office, with lots of maps affixed to its wall. The house also had a kitchen where the men did their own cooking, and there was an adjoining dining area. Tom Colquitt recalls that the floors of the house were mined with guncotton and detonators.

The Section's transport was a platoon truck (with RASC driver) and a Utility (a small van-like vehicle). They did not have bicycles or motorbikes, although a despatch rider (DR) visited occasionally. Lieutenant Pike had his own private car for transport and Capt George Woodward used a Humber Snipe staff car.

All AU Scout Section members were issued with a pass card that had the letters "W.D." and the words "AUXILIARY UNITS" printed on it. This card was their only means of identification as they did not carry *AB64 (Army Service and Pay Book Pt 1 should be in a soldier's possession at all times)* or wear any insignia other than the Royal Norfolk Regiment's cap badge. They made frequent inspections of the AU operational patrols, which they used to refer to as "Home Guard" patrols for security reasons. Their visits were not regular, however, and they never involved an overnight stay.

The East Norfolk AU Scout Section acted independently and apparently had very little interaction with the "Home Guard" patrols, which they regarded as greatly inferior. They felt that the "Home Guard" patrols would act merely as a buffer, allowing the Scout Section to inflict real damage.

The large garden surrounding Beech House was used for general training (but not for explosives exercises) and it also contained one of the patrol's two OBs. The operational base was rarely used for training. Access was through a drop-down shaft, the entrance to which was hidden under a cold frame. The lid lifted and the floor came up, allowing access down a ladder. The main chamber consisted of an L-shaped room measuring about 18 x 9 feet (6 x 3m), with a flat, double-skinned corrugated iron roof and brick built walls. It contained a number of bunks. There was a brick built section that had a concrete roof and a steel door. The latter was used for the storing of arms and ammunition.

The OB was fully equipped with food and ammunition and everything was kept in separate steel boxes, which contained silica packets to keep the stores dry. These stores were kept in separate brick built areas of the OB, as mentioned above approximately six-foot square, which had a concrete roof and floor, and a steel door. The emergency escape passage was two or three feet high and 10 to 20 yards long. It emerged in a nearby copse.

The Section also had a wireless set that was kept in an alcove near the end of the escape tunnel. Tom Colquitt thought that their call sign was "Bowling 9", implicating that the set would have been linked with the SD Branch IN-station at Norwich which used the call sign "Bowling". A more accurate explanation is found in the HQ GHQ Aux Units War Establishment, dated 20 Feb 1941, according to which a Royal Signals OWL (Operator Wireless and Line) was routinely posted in to each Scout Section. The set was battery powered and to be used in an emergency only, and apart from a few brief tests no messages were ever sent.

Tom Colquitt recalls that the Wroxham AU Scout Section members had their own choice of weapons.

> "There was one .22 single shot bolt action sniper rifle and a .303 Lee Enfields, and they also had .38 Webley pistols and .38 Smith & Wessons with lead pistol rounds, rather than nickel. The Thomson submachine gun was preferred to the Sten gun, which they discarded because of frequent jamming.
>
> The patrol also trained with German weapons such as the Mauser pistol, Spandau MG and Potato Masher Grenade. In addition, they were issued with rubber truncheons, brass knuckle-dusters, prismatic compasses and Fairbairn fighting knives made by Wilkinson Sword."

They typically wore the knife on the left hip, along with the holster for the pistol, with the latter's lanyard either being removed or tied to the belt, not around the neck. When crawling through a wood, the pistol was placed down the back of the neck where it was least likely to get snagged. The men wore waterproof rubber ankle boots that allowed silent movement. Tom Colquitt recalls that they did squeak in the wet, though.

The Scout Section had a variety of specialist explosives and other paraphernalia at their disposal. Tom Colquitt remembers:

"There were pull and pressure switches and what we called "debollickers" (castrators). We used Nobel 808 sticks and plastic explosive which could only be made in black and could be shaped into small lumps to hide in the coal of a train engine. We were also equipped with time pencils and 36 detonators, together with 2-feet per minute black fuze and instant HE fuze (composed of PETN - *Pentaerythritol tetranitrate*). We also had specially designed matches with a bulbous red tip and a black body, marked halfway with red band, which glowed, rather than burnt with a flame and that could not be blow out in the wind, called The Fuzzee."

"We also made up our own charges, depending on the target, and on one occasion the patrol devised a booby trap for vehicles and tested it out. A cocoa tin was nailed to a tree, with a 36 grenade (pin removed) wedged inside. A wire then ran from this grenade to another, similarly mounted on the other side of the road. When a vehicle struck the wire it would behave like explosive boleros. Lt. Pike tried this out in his car (with dummy grenades) and was hit in the face when his car's windscreen got knocked down."

The site of East Norfolk Scout Section's OB in the garden of Beech House, Wroxham

The OB was the site of an explosion: a member of the patrol (Bob Butcher) accidentally ignited a gas bottle that had been left switched on and it is thought that an engineer was injured. Capt Woodward consequently issued strict instructions on the use of Calor gas after this - the document (*below*) has survived in the National Archives.

COPY.

Subject:- <u>Safety Precautions - Calor Gas.</u>

<u>G.34/42.</u>

To All Group Commanders.

    Calor Gas <u>may be used with great care.</u>

    Top tap under gas mantle to be permanently turned ON by strapping to pipe with adhesive tape, thereby making certain that main tap on Cylinder is turned OFF when not in use.

    G.Cs. will write to this office confirming that this has been done.

    Extract of H.Q. letter for further precaution as follows:-

    Whenever entering an O.B. in which Calor Gas is installed, the first person will proceed with a torch and inspect the containers to make sure they are properly turned off, and only after having done so will a match be struck.
    Enquiries are being made to find out whether there is any simple test which can be applied to ensure that the air is gas-free, and as soon as this has been ascertained a further communication will be sent to you on this subject.

                      (Sgd.) G. WOODWARD.
         Capt. Cmdg. Auxiliary Units, Norfolk Area.

c/o G.P.O.,
Wroxham,
Norfolk.
13/10/42.

Beech House has long since been converted back into a private dwelling. The OB in the back garden was destroyed only a few years ago. A slight depression and a small heap of bricks remain. Most of the surrounding trees had come down during the Great Storm in 1987. The patrol's second operational base is believed to have been destroyed by construction work for the new Yacht Club on Wroxham Broad.

After the war, the Scout Section regulars were posted back to their regiments and most disappeared without a trace. The fate of only five of them has been documented. In 1943, Tom Colquitt transferred to the Royal Engineers and he was sent to Longmoor where he attended a training course as a railway controller. After further training at the Edinburgh Battle School he sailed for the Mediterranean with Lord Lovat's Scouts. He later served on military railways in Italy and helped run a captured armoured railcar, "The Atom", which ran on a stretch of railway near the Yugoslav border and had precedence over all other traffic. After the war Tom Colquitt joined the Police Force and he later worked as a Fire and Security Officer until his retirement in 1981. He died on 29 May 2010.

Corporal Leslie "Les" Charles Long (Army Number 6019123) joined the Special Air Service (SAS, B Squadron). He was 26 years old when taking part in Operation Bulbasket, where he was captured by the German Army on 3 July 1944 and executed in Foret de Saint-Sauvant on 7 July 1944. He is buried in Rom Communal Cemetery, France, Military Plot Row 1 Coll. grave 1-26.

Private Victor Owen "Chalky" White (Army Number 6011364, formerly Royal Norfolk Regiment) also joined the SAS (B Squadron). Like his colleague from the AU Scouts, Leslie Long, he was one of the men who took part in Operation Bulbasket. He was captured by German troops on 3 July 1944 and executed in Foret de Saint-Sauvant on 7 July 1944. He is buried in Rom Communal Cemetery, France, Military Plot Row 1 Coll. grave 1-26.

After a brief stint as AU IO of Norfolk, Lt Pike joined the Phantoms (GHQ Liaison Regiment).

West Norfolk Scout Section

According to JS Watson of the West Norfolk Scout Section, they operated in an area ranging from Brandon on the Norfolk/Suffolk border to Sheringham in north-east Norfolk and along the cost line from there up to King's Lynn in the west and Swaffham and Fakenham further to the south. All members came from the 2nd battalion Bedfordshire and Hertfordshire Regiment, which had just returned from Dunkirk and was reforming at the Regimental Depot at Kempston, Bedfordshire. A notice was placed on 'Daily Orders', asking for volunteers for a secret operation and all the volunteers were personally interviewed by Staff Officer Colonel Gubbins – the main theme of the interview being the men's ability to live off the land. The men were also told that in case they were selected, the operation was definitely in England but no further information would be given until they had signed the Official Secrets Act, and the following were finally chosen.

> 2/Lt Martin
> Sgt Bell
> Cpl Lambert
> L/Cpl Brown
> Recruit Lewis
> Recruit Jerome
> Recruit Cronk
> Recruit Dickenson
> Recruit McKinley
> Recruit Hullyat
> Recruit JS "Jim" Watson

There was also an RASC driver by the name of Barlow, for the officer. Their first posting was to King's Lynn with the first HQ being in Portland Street. This was an empty house taken over by the War Office. The men were instructed that their duties were to assist in the training of civilian groups of about 10 men in each group, in the art of sabotage and guerrilla warfare. Many of the weapons and explosives, grenades and booby traps etc were not on General Issue in the Regular Army and most had been specially bought in from the USA, such as Thompson machine guns and rifles with telescopic sights. Various members of the Scout Section attended an updating course at Coleshill House where they were instructed in the use of these weapons.

Apparently the West Norfolk Scout Section members were not involved in the construction of OBs for the use of AU patrols they were to instruct. Jim Watson recalls that the hideouts were extremely well camouflaged and one could pass by a yard away without knowing they were there. Out of about 25 or 30 built in their area of West Norfolk, and although training some members of the 20 to 30 patrols, he knew the exact location of only about six and he was unable to later find any of them. According to Jim Watson the hideouts were stocked with arms and explosives and enough food for 14 days, "this being the life expectancy we had if the country was overrun".

Local people were very suspicious of the men because they did not belong to any known unit and they had passes which indicated that no military police or other guards were to question their activities or whereabouts. For this reason they were forced to move HQs frequently. After having moved into the empty house in Portland Street, King's Lynn, in September 1940, in March the following year they moved into a farmhouse in the village of Anmer, on the Sandringham Estate. In late 1942 they made their HQ at another farmhouse, this time in the village of North Creake.

By 1943, the Section had been cut down to just a few regulars and both the Norfolk units were amalgamated into one section. By that time Lt LB Martin who, unusually, had resigned his commission in 1942 and was replaced by Lt FS Meller, had superseded Lt R Clear. The section was further depleted by more postings, leaving only four men. These four were given civilian billets in Burnham Market where they remained until stand-down. L/Cpl A 'Nobby' Clarke from Great Yarmouth, recruit King from Aylsham (both Norfolk) and recruit A Ayres from March, Cambridgeshire – all former members of the East Norfolk Scout Section - were posted back to the Royal Norfolk Regiment, and JS "Jim" Watson, who by then had been promoted to sergeant, went back to his parent unit, the Bedfordshire & Hertfordshire Regiment.

Contrary to the common belief that AU Scout Sections always had two OBs (to accommodate all its members), the West Norfolk AU Scouts only had one, and this they used in shifts: six men on and six men back in billet. This interesting set-up was confirmed to us by Jim Watson, now aged 93.

Although intact, the Scout Section's OB *(see page overleaf for pictures)* is silted up, with sand filling the main chamber and only a crawl space remaining below the curved roof. Access was via a drop-down shaft built of concrete. Wooden posts and boards support the concrete walls. The vertical entrance shaft is adjoined by a narrow passage that would once have been sufficiently high for the men to walk upright through it and into the main chamber. The roof timbers are covered with corrugated sheeting and a layer of concrete, covered with topsoil in order to conceal it. Burrowing rabbits have exposed sections of the exterior walls of the entrance shaft and passage, revealing that they were lined with corrugated sheets on the outside, presumably in an attempt to protect the concrete from getting damp. Both end walls were constructed from corrugated sheets, held in place by wooden posts.

The entrance shaft is covered by a modern steel lid, complete with two handles. The words 'MARBLE ARC" can be seen written into the concrete forming the top outer rim of the entrance shaft. Who wrote them, and why, has as yet to be discovered.

Entrance shaft and passage *(left)* and the silted up main chamber of West Norfolk Scout Section's OB. The exit opening appears to have been cut out of the corrugated sheets forming one of the end walls. An overgrown, trench-like depression in the ground leads away from it, further into the wood. In all probability this was the emergency escape tunnel.

According to Jim Watson, no Royal Signals OWL was attached to his Section and they did not have a wireless set.

Suffolk's Auxiliary Units operational patrols

Map of Suffolk

Norfolk

Fritton x 2
(Norfolk
Group 9)

Beccles

Brandon &
Lakenheath
(Norfolk Group 10)

Wrentham

Metfield

Weybread

Wangford

Holton

Hoxne

Stradbroke

Thorington

Laxfield

Peasenhall

Sibton

Saxmundham

Leiston

Debenham   Framlingham   Stratford
St Andrew

Cambs

Easton

Lt Glemham

Debach

Dallinghoo

?

Hasketon

Gt Bealings

Eyke

Woodbridge

Ipswich #1

Hintlesham

Sproughton

Ipswich #2

Copdock

Capel St Mary

Nacton

Raydon

Bentley

Essex

East Bergholt

By 1941, 180 men had been recruited and 28 patrols had been formed in the County of Suffolk, with one more patrol in the planning. Each of these patrols had their own operational base, with one in the process of being built and another one planned. An undated later list mentions the names of 35 patrols. Five Group Commanders had been appointed. Like all other AU patrols within a region which extended from Northumberland in the north to the Thames-Severn stop line in the south, Suffolk's patrols had been absorbed into "GHQ Special Reserve Battalion 202" by 1943.

The Suffolk AU patrols were divided into five groups, each one named after the largest village or town within their operational area: Group 1 - Beccles Group (five patrols), Group 2 - Metfield Group (five patrols), Group 3 - Framlingham Group (nine patrols), Group 4 - Woodbridge Group (six patrols) and Group 5 - Ipswich Group (nine patrols),

Each one of the groups was made up from a number of AU patrols, ranging from five to nine, and was contained within a (sometimes very roughly) defined geographical area in which the patrols operated. A handful of patrols based in the South Norfolk – North Suffolk border region, such as Brandon and Lakenheath Patrols in the Breckland area, bordering on Norfolk and Cambridgeshire, and Fritton Lake Patrol near Lowestoft in the north-east, were under the command of Capt George Woodward, Intelligence Officer for the County of Norfolk.

The Suffolk AU HQ was housed at the Mill House in Cransford near Framlingham, where Suffolk's Auxiliary Units Scout Section was also billeted until they were stood down in 1943. The house has since undergone several alterations.

Just as in Norfolk, some of the Suffolk patrols were known or referred to under different names. To complicate matters further, auxiliers who all were members of the same patrol sometimes use different names: one might be calling it "Debach" Patrol whereas another would be referring to it as "Clopton" Patrol and a third might know it as "Otley" Patrol.

Although all operational bases were scheduled to be destroyed after stand-down, many of them were never found, and some of them have not been discovered even after almost 70 years, which goes to show just how extremely well hidden they were (and still are). A number of auxiliers recall that the first time they were taken to their patrol's operational base they were told to stop at a certain location and then asked to look around to see if they could spot the entrance. None of them ever did despite the fact that some of them were standing right on top of the trap door.

SUFFOLK GROUP 1 (Beccles)

Beccles Group consisted of five patrols, which were commanded by Lt WDG Bartram, assisted by Lt DJ Proctor who had transferred from Ipswich Group (Suffolk Group 5), where he had been one of GCO Capt EG Pawsey's assistants.

Beccles is a market town in the Waveney District and is located near the South Norfolk – North Suffolk border. It is 26 kilometres (16 miles) south-east of Norwich, and 53 kilometres (33 miles) north-east of the County town of Ipswich. Nearby towns include Lowestoft to the east and Great Yarmouth to the north-east. The patrols operated within a radius of about 20 kilometres (13 miles) from the town.

Beccles Patrol: Sgt Kenny Pink; Pte Cyril "Wag" West; Pte Sonny Spalding; Pte Cecil Cole; Pte Reggie Goffin

Unfortunately, no trace remains of the patrol's operational base which was situated in Worlingham Wood. In all probability the site was destroyed during construction work for the A146 road (Beccles bypass), which links two of East Anglia's largest population centres: Norwich in Norfolk and Lowestoft in Suffolk. Sadly, no patrol members survive to tell where exactly their OB was located and how it might have looked. The 44th Infantry division was based at Worlingham Hall.

Halesworth Patrol: Sgt H Sutherland; Pte RC Norman; Pte Cecil T Mawby; Pte Rex Summerfield; Pte RV Nolloth; Pte AJ Harrison (from Filby, in the Broadland district)

Halesworth Patrol was sometimes also referred to as Holton Patrol, presumably because its operational base was situated in the village of Holton. The hideout was built into the upper edge of a disused gravel pit located in a wooded area in the extensive grounds surrounding the Mill House in Holton. The OB had collapsed at sometime during the 1980s and was subsequently filled in, with a length of twisted iron stanchion marking its location. Fortunately, the owner did take photographs of the interior before the structure was made inaccessible due to health and safety reasons. The main chamber was an elephant shelter set onto concrete plinths, with its end walls built from breezeblocks.

The emergency exit passage, however, is still in place and accessible for most of its length. Its rectangular opening is framed by red bricks and emerges on the slope of the pit. The walls of the breezeblock-built passage are lined with corrugated sheeting. Breezeblocks, one on top of each other and bonded with cement, support a roof of concrete slabs. A layer of soil conceals the tunnel roof on the outside. The patrol's observation post was located nearby, about half way between the Mill House and The Cherry Tree Pub. No trace remains.

Thorington Patrol: Sgt Walter E Thirkettle; Pte WE Charlie "Crown" King; Pte Clifford "Jim" Musk; Pte Herbert Boarder; Pte A John Beck; Pte H Lennie Hackwell

The operational base used by the men from Thorington Patrol was built in a private wood located a couple of miles south-east of the village. It is an elephant shelter that was accessed through a drop-down entrance shaft and it had an emergency exit leading out the opposite end, both long collapsed. The earthen end walls of the dugout were lined with corrugated sheeting much of which has since corroded away. Apart from missing much of both its end walls, the main chamber is dry and intact, albeit very silted up and hence inaccessible. The site is located on a sandy slope and well concealed by a dense growth of bracken. In the 1940s, a now hardly discernible and overgrown track would have been the chosen route of access.

Wangford Patrol: Sgt JF Mallett; Cpl A Bob Hazell; Pte ER Moore; Pte William "Billy" Hazell; Pte GF Bryenton

Wangford Patrol's OB was built near the edge of a wood located on the Henham Estate. It is a very well constructed elephant shelter that is resting on concrete plinths which in all probability would have been used for sitting on. Its end walls and the deep drop-down entrance shaft were built from breezeblocks, and there is some evidence that the trapdoor that originally covered the entrance opening was operated by a counterweight-assisted mechanism. Concrete rubble at the bottom of the shaft indicates that the counterweight shattered when landing on the floor, after the wire holding it in place had corroded.

The main chamber appeared to have been very well ventilated and all the glazed ceramic ventilation pipes seem to still be in situ. The emergency exit passage, however, has collapsed all the way up to the main chamber's end wall, blocking access. This has resulted in soil trickling down into the chamber at the far end. The main chamber is dry and intact and still contains a number of original artefacts including vent covers, a bucket, an aluminium flask, pots and pans and a 1940s Valor Junior No. 56 paraffin heater/stove.

Wrentham Patrol: Sgt WF Routledge (discharged); Sgt Tom A Routledge; Cpl LC "Lennie" Hall; Pte WR Harper; Pte R Gilmour; Pte WGW "Wally" Clark

The patrol's operational base was built on private farmland, dug into the steep bank of a disused pit located within a copse near the hamlet of Wrentham West End. According to patrol member Wally Clark, a retired farm worker and the youngest man in the patrol - and the only surviving member - there had always been a problem with flooding due to the hideout's location very near the bottom of the pit.

Nevertheless, the OB seems to have been in use until stand-down because a replacement operational base was never built. The pit has at some time in the past been transformed into a wildlife pond, in the process of which the OB was damaged by heavy machinery and it is believed to have consequently been removed. A few loose corrugated iron sheets remain on the site.

Stand-down photo depicting members of Auxiliary Units patrols in Beccles Group
(Photo: A Leyneek - Photographer, Maker of Fine Photographs, Amateurs' Supplies & Service)

Back row from left to right:

Herbert Boarder (Thorington); Charles "Crown" King (Thorington); Lenny Hall (Wrentham); Sgt Walter Thirkettle (Thorington); Leonard "Lennie" Hackwell (Thorington); John Beck (Thorington); Reggie Goffin (Beccles); Rex Summerfield (Halesworth)

Middle row from left to right:

Unknown; Unknown; Sgt Tom Routledge (Wrentham); Lt WDG Bartram (Group Commander); Sgt Jack Mallett (Wangford); unknown; Cecil Cole (Beccles); Cyril 'Wag' West (Beccles)

Front row from left to right:
Unknown; Sonny Spalding (Beccles); Billy Hazell (Wangford); George Bryenton (Wangford); Walter "Wally" Clarke (Wrentham)

SUFFOLK GROUP 2 (Metfield)

The village of Metfield is situated close to the border with Norfolk, approximately 11 kilometres (7 miles) north-west of Halesworth, the location of one of Beccles Group patrol's OBs. During the War, an aerodrome was built just outside Metfield. It was used by the USAAF 491st Bomb Group and the 353rd Fighter Group. The local economy is mainly agricultural.

Metfield group comprised five patrols, commanded by GCO Lt Hedley Rusted, a local butcher. Lt Rusted does not appear to have had an assistant. Some of his relatives, brothers or cousins perhaps, can be found amongst the members of various other patrols in this group, two of them in Metfield Patrol.

Hoxne Patrol: Sgt George W Thirkettle (farmer); Cpl Kenneth "Ken" Charles Rush; Pte Gordon Witton (farm worker); Pte Herbert Knight; Pte Arthur J Knight; Pte Gordon E Thirkettle (brother of Sgt GW Thirkettle); Pte WEF Thirkettle

The patrol was formed by Major Raven of Hoxne and, so we were told, was frequently referred to as the "Suicide Squad". Hoxne Patrol's operational base was constructed by the Royal Engineers. It was an elephant shelter located in a private wood near Denham Low Road between Hoxne and Redlingfield. The structure was removed during de-forestation in the 1960s and no trace remains.

Laxfield Patrol: Sgt Peter J Freeman; Cpl Gordon Ayers; Pte F Ray Mann; Pte Fred W Neave; Pte W Garford – left pre 1943 and was replaced by Pte Edward "Ted" George Pipe; Pte Ivan A Smith

The patrol was sometimes also referred to as Ubbeston Patrol. The patrol members' operational base was an elephant shelter buried below the upper edge of a privately owned wood that is growing on a slope above a small stream. The main chamber was accessed via steps leading down to the concealed entrance. The end walls were built from corrugated sheeting held in a timber frame. The structure has since silted up, considerably raising the floor level. Both end walls are missing.

Metfield Patrol: Sgt Vic Seaman; Cpl JW Baxter; Pte Ernest WD Haddingham; Pte W Flatt; Pte K Rusted; Pte M Rusted; Pte Clifford Riches; Pte H Runnacles; Pte KN Runnacles

Metfield Patrol had the code name "Duck". The patrol's operational base is a very solidly built construction consisting of an elephant shelter that is resting on brick foundations. It has brick end walls and a deep, brick-built drop-down entrance shaft with steel rungs set across one corner. The remains of broken concrete counterweights are lying at the bottom of the shaft. The emergency exit passage leading out the opposite end had a roof constructed with corrugated sheeting resting on timbers. The passage too was constructed from red-brick. Its roof has since collapsed but the sheeting is still in situ. Soil has trickled into the chamber through the exposed exit opening, partially blocking the exit passage. The OB contains remains of badly deteriorated bunk beds which were made from wire netting nailed onto a simple wooden frame. No trace remains of the original trapdoors which once covered the entrance shaft and the exit of the emergency passage. A number of glazed ceramic ventilation pipes emerge from the ground above.

The OB is situated in the extensive grounds of Middleton Hall, bounded by a large garden on one side and by a deep gully on the other. At the time it was constructed, the Hall was owned by patrol member Ernest WD Haddingham, a fact that helps explain the relatively close proximity of the hideout to human habitation.

Stradbroke Patrol: Sgt Gordon D Last – he remained in the patrol for only 2 years and was succeeded by Sgt Robert A Pitt; Cpl Ron S Holmes (farm worker); Pte Ivan Mower (joined when only 16); Pte Ralph Clarke (joined at 16); Pte Russel Cattermole (transferred because he was called up); Pte Walter E Marjoram - he was blind in one eye (transferred); Pte A Mower (transferred); Pte Basil Hugman

Stradbroke Patrol's operational base was completed and ready for use by September 1940. It was of flattop construction, built by the patrol members themselves. It is situated near the foot of a disused sandpit close to the edge of a privately owned wood. The main chamber was constructed from timber and corrugated sheeting and it had an adjoining room which housed the bunks. Access was through a trapdoor that was concealed by a wooden tray containing soil. The OB had no emergency escape exit.

The hideout has long since collapsed and a deep rectangular depression denotes the location where it once stood. Some of the corrugated sheeting remains, marking the location of some of the walls. Weathered timbers and wooden posts can still be seen standing near the entrance. Two lengths of dislodged glazed ceramic ventilation pipe are leaning against the collapsed rear wall as if holding vigil.

The patrol members were ill equipped in that their only weapons were knives, and revolvers for which they had one round of ammunition. They trained locally and only once were they invited to attend training further away. Hoping at first that they might go to Coleshill, it turned out, to their great disappointment, that they only went as far as Dunwich beach, 20 miles (30 kilometres) away.

Weybread Patrol: Sgt Richard "Dick" F. Smith; Cpl James Pipe; Pte Dick Matten; Pte Wilfrid G Algar; Pte Walter Matthews; Pte Jim C. Smith; Pte AR Meadows (transferred); Pte SJD Bond

Weybread Patrol's OB was situated near the western edge of a small area of woodland growing on a slope above an unnamed tributary of the River Waveney. The main chamber was an elephant shelter resting on a plinth of either redbrick or concrete. It was accessed through a drop-down entrance shaft with steel rungs in one of its walls. The shaft had a wooden cover that rested on slightly off-centre pivots. It would swing upwards by pulling a steel wire. The chamber's end walls were constructed from corrugated sheeting, held in place by a timber frame. The exit doorway at the far end was off-centre, giving access to an emergency escape passage that had already collapsed in the 1960s. The wood was cut down after the war and the land was transformed into a cattle pasture. The elephant shelter is probably still in the ground, albeit inaccessible. The OB was connected via field telephone to an observation post located within sight, on the edge of the wood. The telephone cable was found buried six inches (15 cm) deep, still in situ, many years later. The patrol is believed to have had a second observation post near the old Shotford Bridge.

All patrol members were local men; Wilfrid Algar and his cousin, Dick Matten, both farmed nearby. Since Auxiliary Units patrols worked under the guise of being members of the Home Guard and wore Home Guard uniforms, the men from Weybread Patrol explained their activities - which often resulted in their being away from home at night and over whole weekends - as being members of the "Home Guard Mobile Squad". *(Not to be confused with the self-styled "mobile squads" some of the Home Guard units had set up, a practice that was discouraged.)*

SUFFOLK GROUP 3 (Framlingham)

Framlingham is a market town located in the Suffolk Coastal District, with the nearest railway stations being in Wickham Market and Saxmundham. Framlingham Group consisted of nine patrols that were well distributed across the region, ranging from Sibton and Peasenhall in the north to the estate village of Easton in the south. The group was commanded by Capt George Scott-Moncrieff, who lived in Hacheston. He was assisted by Lt LWO Turner (Debenham) and Lt Thomas Hamilton Denny (Leiston).

Debenham Patrol: Sgt Rev. Trevor Waller; Cpl AD Aldridge; Pte TH Oxborough (news agent); Pte LC Rowe; Pte Norton G Saunders (bus driver); Pte J Richie (farmed at Poplar Hall); Pte William Edgar Harris (teacher); Pte RC Fisher; Pte Ronald Watson *(he was the local milk roundsman and a member for a short time only)*

Back row from l to r: NG Saunders, Lenny Rowe, Doug Aldridge, RC Fisher, WE Harris
Front row from l to r: Rev T Waller, GCO Capt George Scott-Moncrieff, J Ritchie
(Photo source: Rev John Pretyman Waller)

The Mid Suffolk Light Railway, built at the turn of the century to serve the villages and agriculture of Mid Suffolk, opened in 1904 and was extended in 1906 with the original idea having been to push it across to Southwold and also to join with the East Suffolk Railway which ran via Debenham and Otley to Ipswich. These links, however, were never built and track that had already been laid was lifted during WWI. Because of the light construction, it did not take long for nature and agriculture to reclaim the track bed and within a few years it was almost impossible to trace the route it had once taken. A few scattered overgrown embankments remain and it was one of these embankments that the men from Debenham Patrol chose as the site for their operational base.

The OB appears to have been a homemade affair which was dug into the embankment, from the top down. It consisted of two chambers which were accessed through a drop-down shaft situated between the two. The chambers appear to have had a flat roof with much of the corrugated sheeting still in situ. Corrugated sheeting, held in place by a timber frame, lined the earthen walls. Very appropriately, the roof was supported by sections of railway lines. The structure has since collapsed and a deep depression marks the location of the drop-down entrance shaft, also collapsed. The shaft had earthen walls, lined with corrugated sheeting and held in place by a timber frame. A gully denoting the course of the emergency exit passage leads way from the site down the side of the embankment.

Debenham Patrol's leader, Sgt the Reverend Trevor Waller, was a member of the Waller family that currently holds a 150-year old tradition of one of their sons becoming a vicar, with the current Reverend John Waller being the fifth generation in an unbroken line which began with his great-great grandfather, Charles Waller, who started the tradition in 1833. Thomas Henry Waller took over, followed by his son, Arthur Pretyman Waller. Next in line was Reverend Trevor Waller, who joined Auxiliary Units and became the leader of Debenham Patrol. His son John, the current vicar, appears to be quite a character, describing himself as a "sporting parson" who until a few years ago had spent at least two days each week out hunting and shooting.

Easton Park Patrol: Sgt Richard Hayward (farmer); Cpl SJ Potter; Pte Richard R Pipe; Pte Maurice Springfield; Pte RG Payne; Pte Arthur W Chatfield (farm worker); Pte FV Warren; Pte George Arment Spink (farm worker); Pte Jack Kindred

No railway embankments for the men from Easton Park Patrol - sometimes also referred to as Glevering Patrol, presumably because some of the men came from the nearby hamlet of Glevering. They built their operational base in a small wooded area situated in Easton Park which, at the time, had not long been sold by auction by its owner Lord James Graham, the later Duke of Montrose. "The Wilderness" as it is still called on OS maps is surrounded by a haha *(sunken wall)* so that the royal guests frequently entertained at the folly situated near its edge could enjoy the wide views across the adjoining parkland.

The patrol's operational base is believed to have been built into the haha. Easton Park was then, and still is, surrounded by what is believed to be the world's longest crinkle-crankle wall, built by the 5th Earl of Rochford in the 1830s. The OB situated within Easton Park remains undiscovered and unrecorded, for the time being.

Framlingham Patrol: Sgt GA Nickolds; Pte RH Nickolds; Pte WE Chapman; Pte RHJ Rodwell; Pte CW Fisk

Framlingham Patrol's operational base was located near the edge of Parham Wood, a private wood north-west of the village of Parham. It was an elephant shelter with a drop-down entrance shaft, built immediately above a disused gravel pit. The location affords wide views over the adjoining fields. The structure was removed at some time after the war and the hole was filled in, although a pronounced depression remains in the ground. The patrol's observation post was situated at the wood's edge within sight of the OB. A few sections of corrugated iron sheeting remain.

Leiston Patrol: Sgt Ted Dunn, succeeded by Sgt Baden Cracknell; Cpl Denis George Brown; Pte Ailwyn Churchman; Pte Leonard Churchman; Pte Jack T Snowdon; Pte Harold G Hammett; Pte Cyril F Kemp; Pte Eric W Baldry

The patrol had the codename "Seamew" which is another name for the common sea gull. The men from Leiston Patrol chose an old bomb crater looking much like small gravel pit as the site for their operational base. It was an elephant shelter that contained six bunks, a table and a few chairs, with candles providing the lighting. At the time the hideout was built it would have been situated near the edge of a wood growing adjacent to Sizewell Common, which during the Great Storm in 1987 lost a great many trees. The OB was damaged and subsequently made inaccessible during tree clearance work. An overgrown depression remains.

All patrol members worked for Richard Garrett & Sons, owners of the Leiston Works and manufacturers of agricultural machinery, steam engines and trolleybuses as well as mountings for the 12-pounder guns used by the Navy. It was at Garretts' where the patrol members modified their Sten submachine guns - notable for simple design and low production costs but also for their proneness to accidental discharges – so that the weapon could be used with greater safety in single-shot mode.

Patrol member Jack Snowdon recalls:

> "I was the last man to join the unit and the youngest man to join and like everyone else in the patrol apart from Lt Denny I worked at Garrett's in Leiston in a reserved occupation."

It was the sergeant and childhood friend Baden Cracknell who asked if Jack would be prepared to join.

> "We had the job of testing these Sten guns which were hopeless. We had to modify ours on Garrett's machinery to get them to fire a single shot otherwise they would go off on automatic on their own."

Jack was very surprised when he was taken to see the patrol's operational base:

> "They took me on to Sizewell Common and they stood there talking to me and all of sudden out of the ground, on four little pillars, came about a yard square of turf and when it was lifted up about three feet off the ground on the steel pillars you could walk down a ladder underground. There were six little bunks and the smell of almond - the smell of the explosive. We didn't use much of it until the time came for us to stand down. We took the surplus of the explosive into the countryside and blew a lump out of a tree."

Jack also said that the men were not supplied with suicide pills in case of capture "but we were given a gallon drum *[sic]* of rum to buoy our spirits up. We never drank it - we had to return it. I heard that some other patrols did manage to drink the rum but filled the cask *[sic]* up with tea." After the Auxiliary Units were stood down in 1944, Jack "honestly never talked to anybody" about his service.

Peasenhall Patrol: Sgt WW Kerridge (he kept the Fish & Chips shop in Peasenhall); Cpl JE Simpson; Frederick C Stannard (discharged - moved away through work); Pte RJ Lambert; Pte GWR Thompson; Pte JR Denny

The patrol's operational base was built in a privately owned wood. The site is located on a bank of alluvial deposits of sand and gravel not far from the wood's edge. The main chamber was an elephant shelter with a drop-down entrance shaft and an emergency exit at its opposite end. The course of the collapsed exit passage can still clearly be seen on the ground. It was about eight metres long and emerged on the upper face of a slope. Both entrance shaft and main chamber have collapsed, creating two adjoining crater-like depressions in the ground. One of the end walls appears to still be standing, forming a bridge between the two craters. The estate gamekeeper recalls having seen a bench made from scaffold-like poles supporting a wooden board in the main chamber while it was still accessible less than 10 years ago.

Saxmundham Patrol: Sgt E Charles T Manby; Sgt Fred "Doubles" Woolnough; Sgt Edward "Ted" Woollard; Pte Geoffrey "Stamper" Blake; Pte Reginald FJ "Rex" Chaston; Pte Jack W Richardson; Pte Horace Smith; Pte EJ Emmerson

Saxmundham Patrol was sometimes also referred to as Carlton Patrol. The patrol's operational base was located on the edge of a privately owned wood near the village of Carlton. The main chamber was an elephant shelter with a brick-built drop-down entrance shaft that has since collapsed. Its upper rim is broken and sections of still bonded bricks are lying on top of the in-filled shaft. A short length of glazed ceramic pipe emerges from within the entrance shaft a short distance below ground level. The entrance shaft is adjacent to a noticeable depression in the ground, created by the collapse of the main chamber. Both the brick end walls appear to still be in place and the ground here remains at its original level. A small opening by the exit reveals some of the underlying upper edge of the Nissen hut-type structure as well as some of the bricks forming the end wall. The emergency exit passage, also collapsed, led downhill to the valley of a small stream.

The patrol members were equipped with anti-personnel grenades of plastic appearance which had a length of ribbon attached to the firing pin (probably No. 69 grenades). According to patrol member Rex Chaston, they found that the most difficult part of their "early warning system" which was set up in the vicinity of their operational base was to knock the bottom cleanly off a beer bottle. Once this was achieved, it was simple enough carefully to fit a Mills grenade with safety pin removed inside, to stand the bottle upright in a place where enemy troops were likely to assemble, and offer temptation in the form of a risqué magazine partly underneath. As soon as the bottle was lifted or tipped, the grenade would fall out, giving an enemy search party five seconds to live or die.

Sibton Patrol: Sgt George L Nimmo; Cpl Eric Newson; Pte William McKie (transferred); Pte BA Mann; Pte Wally Paton; Pte Bill Lambert; Pte CWR "Bob" Lambert

Cpl Newson's brother, Morris, remembered many years later how Eric came home one night wearing camouflage gear and with his face still blacked out, explaining that he had been in an exercise at Coddenham, "invading" an Army camp.

The men from Sibton Patrol, like many of their colleagues from other patrols in this group, chose an elevated spot near a private wood's edge for the location of their operational base. The OB is an elephant shelter, resting on a base of red brick, with both end walls as well as the drop down-entrance shaft built from red brick. The (now badly corroded) steel rungs providing access were set across one corner. Both entrance shaft and main chamber are intact and in good condition. A (broken) pipe is in situ, set across one corner of the shaft approximately one metre below ground level. The main chamber houses the original three concrete counterweights required for operating the trap doors. The counterweights were originally covered with a layer of pitch. Two recesses - one on each side of the entrance from the drop-down shaft into the main chamber – accommodate vent pipes that emerge above ground level on either side of the shaft entrance. The emergency exit passage is about six metres (20 feet) long, leading away from the main chamber in a straight line and emerging just above the bed of a small stream which runs along the wood's edge. The operational base was silted up before being excavated by volunteers from the BRO Museum in Parham in the 1990s. The three pivoted counterweights that can now be seen resting against the main chamber's wall were found during excavation work, covered with layers of soil.

Stratford St Andrew Patrol: Sgt. Herman Kindred; Sgt Percy Kindred (patrol leader); Sgt Joe Woodrow (transferred); Pte Alfred "Alfie" Cable; Pte Hector Wade; Pte Arthur Whiting; Pte Stanley Crane; Pte A Dunnet

Like most other operational bases in this group, Stratford St Andrew Patrol's operational base is situated near the edge of a private wood. The main chamber is an elephant shelter which was set onto concrete plinths The structure is threatened by burrowing animals, resulting in the main chamber silting up as time wears on - all the more so since sections of both end walls, formed by corrugated sheeting, are missing. The main chamber once contained fixed bunks which doubled as seats and had folding bunks above them. It was accessed through a trap door hidden beneath a bush. The entrance cover is described as having been a wooden tray filled with soil in order to conceal it. The toilet was situated behind the ladder in the entrance shaft and it had its own ventilation pipe. At the end of the main chamber, at a slight angle, there was a narrow passage of about 6 metres (20 feet) length. The sidewalls of this tunnel had compartments for stores, and a trapdoor concealed under a privet bush at its end. The Stratford St Andrew OB served as an example for the construction of the replica operational base at the BRO Museum at Parham, which is open to the public during museum opening times.

Herman Kindred recalls that Stratford St Andrew Patrol's observation post was built "right on top" of the A12 road at a very strategic point so they were able to see anybody coming from the east or the west, in both directions. They used a periscope for observing. The OP was connected to the hideout by field telephone, using an existing field fence for carrying the current, ie the men joined the telephone cable to ordinary fencing wire. At first they were sceptical as to how this would work but to their great amazement and delight it worked extremely well.

Another member of the Kindred family, Charles Kindred (a cousin of Percy and Herman), ran an OUT-Station for the Special Duties Branch in the same area the patrol operated in. The wireless set was kept in an old shepherd's hut in the Great Glemham area.

Wickham Market Patrol: Sgt Charles Cuthbert; Cpl Ernie W Gilbert; Pte Walter F Ling; Pte W Fuller; Pte EAJ "Ernie" Stewart; Pte Bill Ramsey; Pte Bob G Bird; Pte Peter Stewart

Wickham Market Patrol was also known as Little Glemham Patrol. It had the codename "Thrush". The patrol's operational base was located in a private wood on the Glemham Estate. Although long since inaccessible, the main chamber appears to be still in situ and it has, miraculously, escaped from being damaged by reforestation work. The site presents itself to the casual observer as a very slight hump in the ground and there are no telltale signs that would give away its secret, the buried standard-size elephant shelter hidden beneath it. In fact, the location can only be found by sweeping with a metal detector, the clear signals of which confirm without a doubt the existence of a large structure being buried underground. Sadly, none of the patrol members appear to still be alive and hence it is not known how exactly it looked and who built it.

Wickham Market Patrol, with GCO Capt George Scott-Moncrieff at front centre
(Photo source: BROM Archive)

The breezeblock-built emergency escape passage is all that remains of Halesworth Patrol's operational base which has collapsed in the 1980s and was consequently filled in.

The corrugated iron sheets forming the end walls of Thorington Patrol's OB have fallen out of the timber framing, leaving both ends of the main chamber wide open for soil to trickle in. Both entrance and emergency exit are collapsed and the structure is in the process of silting up.

Glazed ceramic pipe traversing one corner of the entrance shaft at Sibton OB. Steel rungs can be seen set into the opposite corner. They are now too corroded to be used for access. The OB was in the process of silting up before being excavated in the 1990s by volunteers of the BRO Museum at Parham.

View towards the exit doorway at Wangford OB. The adjoining emergency exit passage has collapsed, resulting in soil trickling down into the main chamber which, over time, will silt up and eventually become inaccessible. A ventilation pipe can be seen in situ above the doorway in the rear wall.

Collapsed entrance shaft at Saxmundham OB *(left)* and remains of the emergency exit passage at Debenham Patrol's operational base *(right)*.

The blocked entrance at Stratford St Andrew Patrol's operational base. Both entrance and emergency exit have collapsed and the main chamber is silting up, a process that is exacerbated by burrowing animals.

The remains of Peasenhall Patrol's OB.

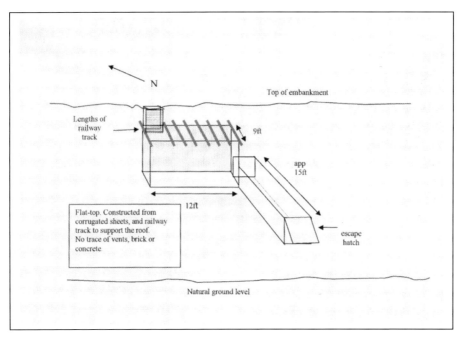

Plan drawing of Debenham OB which was a flattop construction built by the patrol members themselves. It has long since collapsed.

Only a slight depression remains at the site of Leiston Patrol's operational base which had been built into an old bomb crater.

View into the main chamber of Sibton Patrol's OB. It had three pivoted concrete counterweights to operate the trapdoors. The counterweights – they were found covered in layers of soil by volunteers of the BRO Museum in Parham who excavated the OB site in the 1990s - can be seen leaning against the wall *(at left)*.

The site of Wrentham Patrol's operational base. It was damaged and consequently removed. A few corrugated iron sheets mark the location of the OB site.

SUFFOLK GROUP 4 (Woodbridge)

The six patrols in this group operated in the vicinity of the town of Woodbridge, which is located along the River Deben not far from the coast, in the Suffolk Coastal district. The group was commanded by Lt (later Capt) David Walter Beeton (Woodbridge), who worked for W.A. & A.C. Churchman Ltd in Portman Road in Ipswich, manufactures of pipe tobacco, cigarettes and cigars. Later Lt Beeton was employed by the Danish Bacon Company where he worked as a travelling salesman, a job that gave him an excellent excuse for running a small car and to be seen travelling around the area. Capt Beeton's assistant was Lt Marshal Roy Taylor, a farmer who lived at Hasketon Hall.

A record exists according to which the 250th Field Company Royal Engineers under Major ET King MM, RE arrived at a camp in Woodbridge on 8 November 1940. The document further informs that No. 3 Section supervised the defence works in Ipswich, helped building gun emplacements and pillboxes, and erected scaffolding defences on the beach and around the harbour at Felixstowe. Interestingly, the same company had built the elephant shelters for Auxiliary Units patrols in Northumberland and Durham before heading south and could well have been involved in the construction of at least some of the operational bases in the Woodbridge area.

Dallinghoo Patrol: Sgt Jack R Malster (farm worker); Cpl H Jack Garnham (farm worker); Pte Cyril Grimwood; Pte Ernest "Billy" Hood (farm worker); Pte Percy R Neale (farm worker); Pte WH Jarvis; Pte W Fuller

Like many of their colleagues, the men from Dallinghoo Patrol, which, if only to confuse matters, was sometimes also referred to as Pettistree or Bredfield Patrol, chose a disused sandpit located near a quiet country lane for the site of their operational base. It was an elephant shelter with a drop-down shaft and it had an emergency exit passage leading out the far end. The structure was removed many years ago and two massive electricity pylons currently occupy the site. No trace of the operational base remains.

Debach Patrol: Sgt Geoff T Ball; Cpl Sid W Leech; Pte RA Bennett; Pte Tom H Cundy (farmer); Pte HJ Garnham; Pte RJ Chapman

Yet another patrol with several different names, Debach Patrol was also known as Otley or Clopton Patrol. The patrol's operational base was built near the edge of scrubland above Otley Bottom, not far from a footpath. The overgrown spoil heap can still be seen a short distance away, dumped on the edge of a field and now forming part of the scenery. The main chamber was an elephant shelter with a drop-down entrance shaft, the walls of which were lined with corrugated sheeting attached to a timber frame. A toilet cubicle was situated near the emergency exit passage at the far end. Corrugated sheeting was also used for building the chamber's end walls. Unglazed field drain pipes provided ventilation. Sections of these pipes were ploughed up over time and shards can sometimes be found littering the surrounding field.

The scrub has since been cleared and the area is currently an arable field. At some time the OB's entrance and exit have collapsed and the farmer is taking care not to drive his tractor into the two crater-like depressions or over the still intact main chamber so as not to cause any further damage. Needless to say that anybody would have a job getting their tractor out of the hole if it ever got stuck in there. The collapse has resulted in exposing both the chamber's end walls, which, over time, have fallen away. The main chamber is still in situ and access has been blocked at one end. Only a small section of roofline can be seen at the bottom of the crater on the other end. A glimpse inside reveals that the chamber is filled with water reaching almost to roof level.

Eyke Patrol: Sgt CW Carter; Cpl AM Smith; Cpl RG Clark; Pte Roy K Goddard; Pte AM Smith; Pte AS Sage

Eyke Patrol's OB was built near the edge of a private wood adjoining a playing field. It had partially collapsed, with the main chamber apparently still being accessible. As is so often the case nowadays in an age where Health and Safety rules, both entrance and exit openings were blocked only a few years ago in order to prevent children from gaining access, and the County Council workers filled in and levelled the ground above. A slight depression remains above the site, indicating that the main chamber might since have caved in. The course of the emergency exit passage too is visible as a shallow depression.

Great Bealings Patrol: Sgt Henry Stemp (a station master – discharged, possibly due to railway work); Pte Victor Stemp (son – transferred); Cpl E Sidney Read; Pte Ray Read (son – transferred); Pte Barney Steward (he replaced Ray Read); Pte Edward Charles "Ginger" Porter; Pte Derek Pearce; Pte HG Wells

Great Bealings Patrol's operational base was dug in small private wood surrounded by fields on all sides. It was an elephant shelter built by the Royal Engineers and was accessed through a drop-down entrance shaft, lined with corrugated sheeting. An emergency escape tunnel existed at the far end.

Initially the patrol had a problem with ventilation; when ordered to stay in their OB for 24 hours to test it, the candles repeatedly went out because of lack of oxygen, and one after the other of the men eventually stumbled out very much in need of fresh air – some collapsing into a bed of nettles, others clinging to trees to stay upright and vomiting. After this narrow escape the ventilation was improved and the vent outlets were hidden in hollow tree trunks. The OB was filled in during the late 1940s and no trace remains. An observation post is believed to have been located nearby.

Nacton Patrol: Sgt Bill S Milne; Cpl Alfred Edward "Ted" Farrow; Pte Tim (JS) Mann; Pte William R "Bill" Mann; Pte Ted G Buxton; Pte Frederick H Brown

The men from Nacton Patrol had their operational base built in Lady Wood. It was an elephant shelter with its entrance concealed under a bush near the edge of a pond.

Mrs Gillian Bence-Jones of Orwell Park Estate recalls that the main chamber was built with green wood and had always been a concern to her and the family because the children used to play in it. When the ponds were dredged for the fishing club she ordered that the digger give the roof a good 'thump'. This order was carried out and it collapsed quite easily. Mrs Bence-Jones never actually went inside it but says she understood that it was "quite big". She knew it as the 'Home Guard Headquarters'.

For many decades corrugated sheeting, protruding from the ground where the main chamber hidden underneath it had collapsed, marked the location of the OB site.

According to the estate manager, the wood was extensively damaged during the Great Storm in 1987, leaving only six trees standing. The hideout was further damaged by heavy machinery during tree clearance work and subsequently removed. The hole was filled in and nothing remains on the ground. The patrol's ammunition store (or it might have been their observation post) was situated nearby, but this site too has been destroyed and hence the exact whereabouts of both the OB and the OP sites are now lost.

All our attempts to establish the exact location of the sites were blocked by the manager of the Orwell Estate, the only landowner in the whole of Norfolk and Suffolk to refuse access onto their land for the purpose of establishing the exact whereabouts of their local Auxiliary Units patrol's operational base.

We have, however, succeeded in finding the patrol's ammunition store. Most unusual and perhaps unique, a beach hut which was owned by one of the patrol members and is still owned by his family served this purpose. After spending four years in the woods on the Orwell Park Estate, the hut was taken back to its original location on Felixstowe beach after the war, and there it still stands, none the worse for its wartime excursion.

The above picture of Nacton Patrol is believed to have been taken near their OB site (*above – photo source: BROM*). The beach hut that was used as the patrol's ammunition store *(below)* in 2012.

Woodbridge Patrol: Sgt RJ Brooks; Cpl WHJ Brooks; Pte WT Banyard; George H Piper; Pte FH Warren; Pte B Wright; Pte Thomas A Piper; Pte C Adlam (transferred)

Woodbridge Patrol's operational base was built into the side of a sandpit located in the grounds of Melton Grange in Woodbridge. The Grange was surrounded by extensive parkland, bounded by Bredfield Road in the west and by Pytches Road in the south - an area which has since been redeveloped and extensively landscaped, with a new housing estate having been built over it. The patrol's OB was an elephant shelter with a drop-down entrance shaft and an emergency exit tunnel at the opposite end. The entrance was secured with a hinged trap door. A wooden tray in which grass was growing to conceal it covered the trap door. The hideout was destroyed in the course of construction work for the new housing estate which now covers the whole area.

The patrol used one of the ancient trees growing along Love Lane, a footpath that turns off Pytches Road opposite the Woodbridge Clinic, as their observation post. From there they had a good view across the park and towards their operational base. A shelf bracket assisting with access is believed to still be embedded in the tree's trunk.

The Army supplied the materials required for building the ammunition store, a quarter-length Nissen hut. The structure was situated in GCO Lt Beeton's private garden and built by Lt Beeton with the help of members of his family.

The patrol members were issued with Sten guns and they appear to have been well stocked regarding explosives. Explosives, ammunition and weapons were collected and returned after stand-down but other paraphernalia, such as the large magnets commonly used in combination with plastic explosives, were left behind. These magnets were extremely popular amongst boys and a great number of them were sold to schoolmates by some of the patrol members' sons who had found them.

Two mystery OBs

Capt Andrew Croft arrived in Suffolk some time before August 1940, after having set up the first AU patrols in Essex. The first operational bases were frequently nothing more than rectangular dugouts hidden in woodland, with roofs of corrugated sheeting which was supported by lengths of railway tracks, sleepers or timbers. Many of these structures had barely room to house the five patrol members it was intended for, and when the number of patrol members was increased from five to seven in spring 1941, many OBs had to be abandoned for this reason alone. Some patrols had three or even four different bases during the first few months of their existence, one after the other abandoned because they were unsuitable for even short-term use until replacement bases were constructed from a standard drawing. Occasionally this first standard base also had to be abandoned, because it was discovered by school children, courting couples or poachers.

It is therefore not all that unusual to occasionally find one or two more OB sites than there were patrols in any one of the areas covered by AU patrols. In this context it should, however, also not be forgotten that some patrols were disbanded before stand-down and the names of some of these patrols' members were never recorded, and that hence not every "spare" OB is necessarily one of two (or more) serving the same patrol. It could well have been the operational base of an as yet unknown patrol.

OB site near Hasketon Hall

A private diary written by Lt Marshal Roy Taylor, GCO2 of Woodbridge Group and farmer at Hasketon Hall, contains a record of there having been an operational base near the edge of a private wood that is bordering the farm's arable land. Lt Taylor describes the structure as an elephant shelter and he says that it was built by the Royal Engineers. Apparently the structure soon became waterlogged and hence unusable, and it appears to have been destroyed shortly after the war. By the time Lt Taylor's son was old enough to be taken to the site there was nothing left to see. But whose OB was it?

Perhaps this was the first OB of the Woodbridge Patrol, who moved on to the grounds of Melton Grange once it had become obvious that the structure was uninhabitable. Hasketon Patrol is not mentioned in a list containing the names of altogether 34 Auxiliary Units patrols operating in Suffolk, a list that appears to have been circulated to all Suffolk GCOs. Lt Taylor, however, recalls: "we had patrols at Clopton, Hasketon, Great Bealings, Bredfield, Pettistree and Eyke" – Woodbridge Patrol is missing, unless it was the same as Hasketon Patrol and everybody at the time knew this. Perhaps Hasketon Patrol did indeed exist but was disbanded before stand-down, and patrol members' names were hence never recorded. Other patrols operating in the vicinity were Debach aka Clopton or Otley Patrol in the north-west and Great Bealings Patrol in the south-west. Technically, and geographically, the OB site near Hasketon Hall could have been built and used by either of them.

Lt Taylor's list of the patrols in his Group highlights yet again the problem, encountered on a fairly regular basis, which is that some patrols were known to different people under various different names. Without a doubt, the men involved at the time knew exactly who they were talking about - something that can not always be said concerning accounts that were published decades later.

OB site near Foxborough Hall

Whereas the location of the OB near Hasketon Hall allows for an educated guess, at least, the operational base situated near Foxborough Hall Farm, now home of the Suffolk Wildlife Trust, provokes rather more questions than it provides answers. The main chamber is an elephant shelter, built in an area of woodland surrounded by fields, not far distant from a farm track. Both drop-down entrance shaft and emergency exit passage have collapsed, with much of the corrugated sheeting lining the earthen walls of the entrance shaft still in place. The end walls of the main chamber were also constructed from corrugated sheeting, held in place by a timber frame. Once the end walls had become exposed because of the collapse of the adjoining entrance shaft and exit passage, large sections have, over time, fallen away. This has resulted in the main chamber silting up. Soil has trickled into the main chamber, finding its way easily through the large gaps in both end walls. The floor level in the main chamber is now considerably higher than it used to be. A glazed ceramic ventilation pipe is in situ, emerging into the chamber immediately beside the entrance doorway.

Two teenage poachers discovered the site in 1943. The boys had been in the wood in the hope of catching a few rabbits for the pot when they came upon what appeared to be a manhole cover. Whilst still wondering what on earth it might do here in the middle of the woods, they heard male voices emerging from below, and then they ran away.

Apparently the patrol members had, against implicit instructions, neglected to conceal the trapdoor, which, had it been invisible, would not have given cause for the boys to linger above for long enough to hear the occupants' voices.

Assuming the men were aware of the unwelcome visitors and of the fact that their hideout had been discovered, they would have had to move on and build another OB elsewhere. Hopefully time will tell which patrol it belonged to. Geographically, the OB is situated within the area that was covered by patrols of the Woodbridge Group: Debach Patrol (aka Clopton or Otley Patrol); Woodbridge (aka Melton Park) Patrol; Nacton Patrol; Eyke Patrol; Great Bealings Patrol and Dallinghoo (aka Pettistree or Bredfield) Patrol. The location is also only about 5 kilometres distant from a known Scout Section site in the village of Martlesham.

It is possible that this structure served as their second OB. Scout Sections comprised 12 men and for this reason two OBs per Section would normally have been required.

Elephant shelter near Foxborough Hall. The end walls have fallen off the timber frame that held them in place and soil his trickling into the main chamber, silting it up. A glazed ceramic vent pipe can be seen emerging into the chamber beside where the entrance doorway would once have been.

Group photo depicting AU patrol members from the Woodbridge Group at stand-down. GCO Capt David Walter Beeton can be seen in the front row *(centre),* with assistant GCO Lt Marshal Roy Taylor sitting on his right. *(Photo source: Michael Beeton)*

Overgrown site of Dallinghoo OB in a disused sandpit near Byng Bridge.

Exposed roof of elephant shelter with its end wall missing, as seen from the collapsed entrance (Laxfield Patrol).

Ivan Mower, member of Stradbroke Patrol, at the site of his patrol's collapsed operational base where some remains, including corrugated sheeting, timber posts and a section of a glazed ceramic ventilation pipe *(foreground right)* are still in place.

The Weybread "Home Guard Mobile Squad", as they used to refer to themselves, taken in 1942. *(Photo source: Mary Whattam)*

Back row L to R: Cpl James "Jim" Pipe – Pte Wilfrid G Algar – Sgt "Dick" Smith
Front row L to R: Pte AR Meadows – Pte Jim Smith – Pte Dick Matten

Love Lane in Woodbridge, where the patrol's OP used to be up one of the ancient trees along the path *(left)* and the collapsed emergency exit passage at Metfield Patrol's operational base *(right)*.

Remains of end wall at Debach Patrol's operational base. The collapsed entrance shaft has created a deep crater exposing the end wall. The main chamber, an elephant shelter, is filled with water up to almost roof level.

The main chamber of Metfield Patrol's OB, looking towards the emergency exit passage which has collapsed. Soil is trickling into the chamber from above. Over time the chamber will fill in and become inaccessible if no measures are being taken to stop the process.

SUFFOLK GROUP 5 (Ipswich)

Patrol leaders and assistants, with GCO and GCO2 *(at centre front row)* in Ipswich Group
(Photo source: Michael Anderton)

Back row left to right:

Sgt Dennis Johnson (Raydon aka Stratford St Mary Patrol), Sgt Horace Clements
(Copdock aka Belstead Patrol), Sgt Rex Milner Moore (Hintlesham Patrol), Sgt Peter
Hutton (Bentley Patrol) Sgt Neville Devonshire (East Bergholt Patrol), Sgt Jack Chaplin
(Wenham aka Capel Patrol)

Front row left to right:

Sgt Neville Palmer (Ipswich II Patrol), unknown, Lt Eric Pawsey (GCO2), Capt HE
Mellor (GCO), Sgt WR Beaumont (Sproughton aka Burstall Patrol), Sgt LE Hudson
(Ipswich I Patrol)

Copdock Patrol - patrol leader Sgt Horace Clements at front centre, Cpl Reg Airey on his left.

East Bergholt Patrol - back row from left to right: Bill Miller, Cpl Ray Abbott, Charlie Ambrose
Front row from left to right: Billie Smith, Sgt Neville R Devonshire, Charlie Goodchild
(Source of both photos: British Resistance Organisation Museum Archive, Parham)

The patrols in Ipswich Group were the first to be set up in Suffolk by Capt Andrew Croft (then IO for Essex, Norfolk and Suffolk) in the autumn of 1940. The patrol members themselves built the majority of the operational bases used by the patrols in the group. This is another rather large group, composed of altogether nine patrols that, as the name implies, operated in the vicinity of Suffolk's County town Ipswich, located on the estuary of the River Orwell.

The GCO was Capt EG Pawsey of Ipswich, assisted by Lt Harry Edmund Mellor (Ipswich) and Lt CJ Proctor, who at some later time transferred to Beccles Group where he served as one of GCO Lt WDG Bartram's assistants. Lt HE Mellor worked for the Alliance Insurance Co at Ipswich. He moved to Oxford after the war.

Ipswich Group Headquarters – Jermyn's Farm

Although it was fairly common practice for patrols in the same group to attend training exercises together, the locations of their OBs was commonly never revealed to others, and group meetings, especially in the early days, were usually held at the GCO's house. The patrols of Ipswich Group, however, had their own headquarters, basically a safe meeting place in form of a purpose-built fortified cellar that was situated beneath the patio right next to Jermyn's farmhouse. At the time Jermyn's Farm was tenanted by patrol member Bill Church's family and occupied by Jack Hammond, one of their farm workers.

The cellar was accessed through a drop-down shaft built from red brick and concrete. Because the shaft was built within the main chamber it created two recesses to each side of it. In all probability the entrance, or rather the top half of it was deliberately designed to look like a manhole. The actual entrance into the chamber was through a gap between the ceiling of the cellar and the manhole's concrete floor, and it would in all probability have been secured with a hinged lid. Viewed from the interior, the construction forming the bottom half of the entrance shaft looks like a concrete cupboard with a concrete top – the manhole's floor.

The main chamber measures 2.40 x 3.40m (7ft 10 inches x 11 feet). Its flat concrete roof is supported by three 15 x 15 cm (6"x 6") RSJs which sit on top of vertically placed RSJs used for reinforcing the walls. The roof and some sections of the sidewalls were shuttered using 3-inch profile corrugated sheeting. The floor is concrete. Two short sections of railway sleepers, each about 40 cm (15 inches) long and approx 1.60m (5.2 feet) apart, can be seen embedded in the concrete floor near the entrance. What purpose they served is unclear.

The chamber is approximately 2m (6.6 ft) high. The red-brick walls are reinforced by sections of RSJs, embedded in a 10 cm (3.9 in) thick layer of concrete up to a height of about 1.65m (5.2ft). The brick walls extending above this height are exposed. Because of the greater thickness of the reinforced lower sections of wall, a roughly 10 cm wide shelf was created, providing ample storage room. This shelf runs along the whole length of three of the walls. The wall accommodating the entrance shaft and a recess on each side of it does not have a shelf Walls and ceiling were originally painted white. The remains of a hand basin, backed with white tiles, can be seen in the NE corner, and what appears to be a mains water pipe (with tap missing) can be seen partially embedded in concrete on the wall above it. Beside the sink is what appears to have been a wooden shelf.

A 30 x 20 cm (11.8 x 7.9 in) rectangular chute-like opening in the wall nearest the farmhouse just below the ceiling appears to have served as a vent. As far as can be established, after several alterations both to house and garden, the structure was not covered by soil and to the casual observer would have appeared to be a small concreted-over area with a manhole set into it. It may originally have been covered by a cold frame or similar.

Considering that it was built 70 years ago, the structure is in very good condition and well protected by the paved patio above, with a new steel lid securing the entrance shaft. The steel elements reinforcing roof and walls have accumulated a layer of rust, as can be expected to happen over time. The wooden boards affixed to the sidewalls of the entrance shaft are badly deteriorated.

Bentley Patrol: Sgt Peter J Hutton (farmer in Copdock); Sgt William "Bill" Sage Ratford (transferred); Cpl Lionel Crown (Bentley); Pte Gerald Sporle (transferred); Pte Tony GF Hutton (farmer in Copdock); Pte Hugh George Dunt (killed in road accident); Pte MG Miller; Pte Hammond N Betts (farmer)

Bentley Patrol's OB was built in a privately owned wood west of the village of Bentley, not far from a footpath. Evaporated incendiary devices could still be found scattered about on its floor long after it had been abandoned at stand-down. Not all that surprising, considering that according to patrol members' accounts the men had half a ton of gelignite and a great number of hand grenades, fuses and detonators stored in a nearby ammunition dump. The main chamber has long since collapsed with a large rectangular depression marking the location. It appears to have been a flat-topped construction that was built by the patrol members themselves. It was accessed through a drop-down entrance shaft the walls of which were lined with corrugated sheeting, and corrugated sheeting was also used to line the earthen walls of the main chamber. A nearby observation post was connected to the OB via a field telephone line.

The patrol members were well equipped with arms and ammunition, including a submachine gun, a sniper rifle with telescopic sights, revolvers, grenades and 150 rounds of ammunition per man. They trained mainly in sabotage for which purpose they had fuses and detonators and, of course, explosives. They regularly acclimatised themselves to staying underground by spending a full 24 hours in their operational base. In order for the men to be able to do so the structure must have been well ventilated.

Patrol leader Sgt Bill Ratford attended a training course held at Coleshill as did his fellow patrol member Hammond Betts. The patrol members also frequently went out to test the security at nearby Wattisham aerodrome, where one day they got caught and arrested just after they had symbolically 'destroyed' the bomb store. Nothing much came of the arrest, however. Patrol members commonly carried a document advising not to question the document holder but to ring a given phone number instead.

Interestingly, the auxiliers from Bentley patrol not only helped digging the group's headquarters, a fortified purpose-built cellar at Jermyn's Farm in Capel St Mary but apparently they also helped by digging Capel Patrol's operational base and ammunition store.

Copdock Patrol: Sgt Horace Clements; Cpl Reg Airey; Pte Robin Cousins; Pte Derek P Young (he later became a scrap metal dealer); Pte Ralph E Vince; Pte Walter W Hammond; Pte Cyril A Rudland; Pte Frank Jarrold

The patrol was sometimes also referred to as Belstead Patrol. The patrol's operational base was situated in a private wood known as Baldrough's Wood in the 1940s. It was built by the patrol members themselves and on higher, dry ground, roughly in the middle between two forest tracks. The wood has since been felled and the area was replanted with new trees. The OB was either damaged or removed during afforestation work. No trace of it remains.

Sadly, none of the men who used it gave a description as to how it would have looked or how it had been built, although one of the patrol members' accounts at least mentions the weapons they were equipped with: Commando knives, revolvers, a Sten gun and a Thompson submachine gun.

East Bergholt Patrol: Sgt Neville R Devonshire (factory worker from East Bergholt); Sgt Charlie Goodchild (smallholder from Holton St Mary – he was the Home Guard's driver as he was allowed petrol or petrol coupons); Pte WW Bill "Jock" Miller (farmer in Holton St Mary); Pte Ray P Abbott (painter and decorator from Raydon, discharged 14.4.1943); Pte WM Smith (East Bergholt); Pte Charlie R Ambrose (factory worker from Holton St Mary)

The patrol had the codename "Song thrush". The men from East Bergholt Patrol built their operational base in a lightly wooded area known as The Commons, not far from an old cart track. Some of the original sweet chestnut trees can still be seen growing in the area.

The hideout was a flat-topped construction with the roof having been built from corrugated sheeting that rested on sections of disused Ipswich tramlines. The structure has either collapsed or was removed after the war. The location is denoted by a shallow depression, with two lengths of glazed ceramic drain pipes that are cemented together resting on its edge.

Hintlesham Patrol: Sgt Edward Reginald "Rex" Milner-Moore (Fisons Ltd director); Cpl GW Crane; Pte Roy (Raymond) L Double; Pte Geoffery J Urpeth (typewriter salesman); Pte COP "Claude" West (builder); Pte Peter Steward

Patrol leader Sgt Rex Milner-Moore was one of the directors of Fisons Ltd - a leading pharmaceutical, scientific instruments and horticultural chemical manufacturer, founded in 1843 by Edward Packard. He was also an accomplished cricket player and participated in Suffolk Minor Counties Championship matches from 1936 to 1938.

The patrol's operational base was situated in a shed in the extensive garden of Milner-Moore's property on the outskirts of the village of Hintlesham, which he had acquired in 1936. According to patrol member Roy Double the shed was never used in the manner OBs were intended to be used, and the men never spent any time in it. Almost 70 years later the shed still stands, albeit very much overgrown, with the ivy probably being the main reason that it has as yet not fallen apart. Much of the roof has collapsed. The concreted floor had once been covered with wooden boards that have over the years rotted away. An examination of the floor revealed that the boards were not laid down in order to perhaps hide a concealed trapdoor leading into a cellar. What appears to be a double bunk is still in place in one corner. The reason why an above-ground structure was chosen is unclear - unless the men's idea was to hide their OB in plain sight.

Suffolk's County town Ipswich had not one but two patrols that were based in its immediate proximity. They were named Ipswich I and Ipswich II.

Ipswich I Patrol: Sgt LE Hudson; Cpl LH Proctor; Pte SAW Day; Pte EEH Fenn; Pte Edward Kitchener Ransby; Pte LJ Read; Pte HT Sims

Ivan Ransby, son of patrol member Edward Kitchener Ransby recalls:

> "My father lived at Westleton until October 1940 and then moved to Ipswich where he lived until he died in 1992. At some point during the war he worked at Southwold, he told me that he often cycled (yes, cycled) home to Ipswich on a Friday night and then back again on a Monday. At the back-end of the war he was working as a dragline driver for the Catchment Board. At the end of the war he was working at Felixstowe when he was asked to drive a dragline digger for Rogers Bros which he did and he spent the rest of his working life with them."

No information is available concerning the location of the patrol's operational base, which is believed to have been situated on the northern edge of the town, perhaps near the village of Bramford.

Ipswich II Patrol: Sgt Neville G Palmer (Solicitor's clerk); Pte Bruce Wharton; Pte Donald A Gould; Pte John T "Paddy" Langford; Pte Claude Riches (joined in 1942); Pte Len R Whurr; Pte Jack E Hadley

Claude Riches, who was still alive in spring 2013, recalls that their OB was in a wooded area about half a mile south of Ipswich railway station. It was an elephant shelter built by Royal Engineers and about 25 ft long, divided into two chambers, one being used for sleeping in. Ammunition was stored in the OB. The patrol did not have a lookout post (OP). The area was much frequented by dog walkers and access was difficult at the best of times, and therefore the hideout was not used very often. The area has since been built over with houses and the OB was destroyed in the process.

Raydon Patrol: Sgt Dennis Johnson (farmer in Holton St Mary); Cpl Jack Moore; Pte James Hawes; Pte George Rose

Comprising only four members, Raydon, also known as Stratford St Mary Patrol, was the smallest patrol in the whole group. The patrol members chose a disused sandpit - one of several in this area and well off the beaten track - as the site for their operational base. In the 1940s, the pit was surrounded by mature woodland, with many of the trees being elms that later fell victim to the Dutch elm disease. The OB was built into the slope of the pit, about halfway up, overlooking the track leading past it a short distance away.

The main chamber is a flattop construction that was in all likelihood built by the patrol members themselves. The men used a variety of materials available to them including sections of railway line, wooden timbers and posts, corrugated sheeting and what appears to be a sawn off section of telegraph pole. The structure was accessed through a drop-down entrance shaft lined with corrugated sheeting. It had rungs nailed across the corner support for easier access. The operational base had an emergency exit of a short adjoining passage leading out of the pit and into the adjoining field above.

The main chamber is partially collapsed and silted up but much of the corrugated sheeting that formed the roof and lined the earthen walls is still in place, albeit some of it badly corroded. The roof was supported by sections of railway line or disused Ipswich tramline, resting on a variety of sturdy posts, one appearing to be a section of telegraph pole. The corrugated sheeting lining the walls is held in place by a wooden frame. A glazed ceramic pipe protrudes from the ceiling at an angle and a tin pipe of about 7.5 cm (3 inch) diameter is in situ beside the collapsed entrance shaft. Extending upwards and through the roof, its exterior end is capped with an elbow. Presumably it served as a flue pipe for a stove that the patrol had kept in their OB. The site remained undiscovered for almost two decades, only to be found by coincidence in the 1960s, when the landowner only just avoided driving over it with heavy machinery in the course of tree clearance work. By then the entrance shaft and part of the roof had already collapsed.

The patrol members had created a small dugout in the main chamber's floor which they used for storing small quantities of ammunition and fuses. They were equipped with .303s which had been adapted (sleeved) to take .202 ammunition for practice, a couple of Sten submachine guns and grenades, and each had a .38 Smith & Wesson revolver and a Commando knife. The patrol's main ammunition store was situated in another disused pit about 500 metres further along the track leading past the pits. No trace remains of this structure, which is described as having been a square dugout which was covered with a flat roof constructed from corrugated sheeting. An observation post was located within sight of the OB. It was originally hidden within a large hollow tree trunk and it remained hidden for decades, to be discovered only after the tree trunk had deteriorated and fallen on its side.

Sproughton Patrol: Sgt WR Beaumont; Cpl Jack N Gray; Pte BA Batley; Pte CH Beaumont; Pte FC Green; Pte EJ Keeble; Pte JR Meyer

The patrol was sometimes also referred to as Burstall Patrol, presumably because of their operational base being located near the village of Burstall. The OB is situated near the edge of a private wood, a short distance away from a footpath. During the 1940s the land was owned by Burstall Hall. Horse pastures surrounded the wood. The OB is described as having been a fairly large affair that apparently consisted of two buried Nissen huts that adjoined each other at an angle, making the structure L-shaped. The main chamber had a drop-down entrance shaft and the emergency exit passage lead off into the woods at an angle. The structure has long since collapsed and the farmer filled in the depression about 20 years ago. Only a very shallow depression remains on the ground. One of the glazed ceramic vent pipes is still in situ, emerging to ground level from in-between gnarled tree roots which are in the process of crushing it.

Wenham Patrol: Sgt PJ "Jack" Chaplin; Cpl Charles A Coe (he is corporal in 1944); Pte Charles Goddard (left AU in 1943 to join the Royal Navy); Pte TW "Bill" Church (tenant farmer at Jermyn's Farm, Capel St Mary); Pte Len C Wyartt; Pte Walter Pittock (transferred)

The patrol is sometimes also referred to as Capel St Mary Patrol. The men from Capel built their operational base in a spinney near the footpath that runs along the boundary between Jermyn's and Grove Farms. At the time both farms formed part of the Wenham Estate and were worked by tenant farmers. Ipswich Group's headquarters, a safe meeting place for members from all patrols in this group, had already been built at Jermyn's farmhouse, which is located on the other side of the adjoining field and would have been well within sight of the operational base.

The OB had a flat roof constructed with corrugated sheeting, and a wooden entrance shaft. Apparently pulling a ring attached to a chain near a tree stump opened the trapdoor. When pulled, the hatch would swivel open, pivoting in the centre. The earthen walls of the main chamber were lined with corrugated sheeting and the men had a stove for heating and cooking because the structure is described as having had a chimney. The operational base was partially destroyed after the war and only a depression remains today.

The patrol's ammunition store was located a short distance further along the path. A small round depression marks its location.

Picture of Wenham Patrol, taken on 15 October 1944:
Pte Len C Wyartt – Sgt PJ Jack Chaplin – Cpl Charles A Coe – Pte Bill Church
(Picture source: Mrs J Cutting)

A deep rectangular depression marks the location where Bentley Patrol's operational base once stood in a private wood near the village of Bentley.

A glazed ceramic ventilation pipe in the process of slowly being crushed by tree roots which would once have served to conceal where it emerges to ground level, marks the location of the long-since collapsed Sproughton OB.

The overgrown garden shed which served as Hintlesham Patrol's OB.

The site of East Bergholt Patrol's operational base. It was destroyed at sometime after the war. A rectangular depression and a length of ventilation pipe mark the location which is not far distant from an old cart track.

Chimney pipe emerging near the collapsed entrance of Bentley Patrol's OB *(left)*. Sections of tramlines and telegraph poles were only some of the materials used in the construction of Bentley OB *(right)*.

The patio at Jermyn's farmhouse under which Ipswich Group's fortified safe meeting place was built. The manhole cover *(foreground right)* covers its entrance.

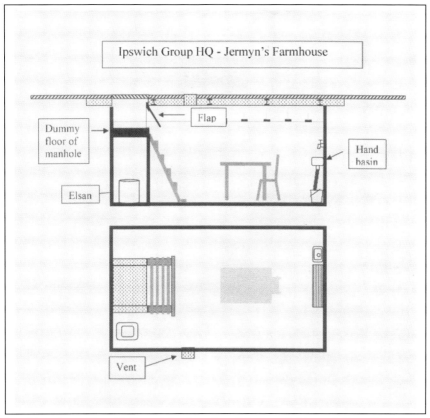

Side and top views of Ipswich Group's headquarters. It is concealed beneath the patio at Jermyn's farmhouse.

Ipswich II Patrol
with patrol leader
Sgt Neville G Palmer
at front centre
(Photo source: BROM)

Only a depression in the ground remains on the site of Wenham Patrol's OB in a spinney near Jermyn's and Grove Farms.

Suffolk Auxiliary Units Scout Sections

Little is known about this Scout Section, apart from that it was commanded by Lt "Mac" McIntyre, assisted by Jack Steward. Other names associated with this Scout Section are Cyril Hall, Geoff Bowery, "Slogger" Leach, Ralph Bailey, Oliver Bloomfield and Joe Middleditch. They men were billeted at the Mill House in Cransford, which also served as the Suffolk AU headquarters. From 1941 onwards Capt JW Holberton was the Suffolk IO.

Virtually nothing is known about the Suffolk Scout Section members. Geoff Bowery recalls that he was more or less ordered to volunteer. At stand-down they would have rejoined their Regiment but it is believed that some of the men moved on to join other forces. Cyril Hall, for instance, served with the Chindits in Burma, the largest of the allied Special Forces of WW2. They were formed and lead by Major General Orde Wingate DSO and operated deep behind enemy lines in North Burma in the War against Japan. Interestingly, by that time Capt Mike Calvert, whom we have already met back in 1940, when he was in Kent helping Peter Fleming with the setting up of the "XII Corps Observation Units", also served with the Chindits, commanding the 77th Indian Infantry Brigade in "Operation Thursday".

The Suffolk Scout Section comprised a dozen men, all from the Suffolk Regiment, who were specially selected and trained. Besides keeping themselves fit through lots exercise they helped to train AU patrols and constructed at least one OB for their own use.

With each section comprising a dozen men, ideally, two OBs were required per section to accommodate all of them, but one of the Norfolk Scout Sections only ever had one, and this they used in shifts. Suffolk's Scout Section OB was a flat-topped concrete structure, situated in a small wooded valley near the village of Martlesham. No trace has been found. Their second OB might have been an as yet unidentified and unassigned dugout found in a wood near Foxborough Hall, about five kilometres distant *(see p 132)*.

Mill House, Cransford, in 2012

Members of the Suffolk Scout Section in front of Mill House *(Photo source: Geoff Bowery)*

Stand down – 1 Nov 1944

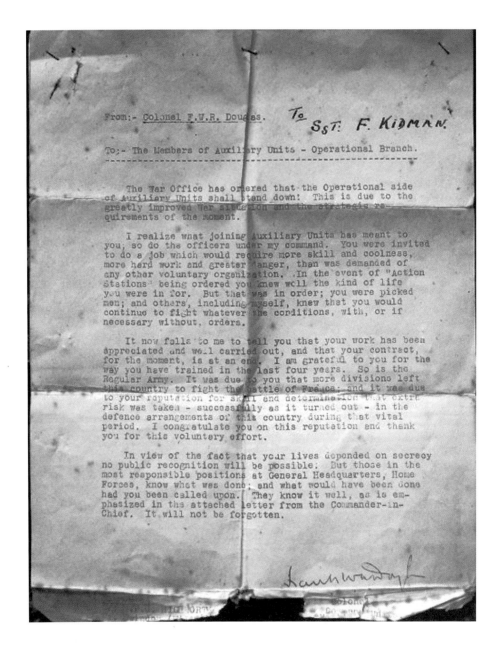

From:- Colonel F.W.R. Douglas.   To Sgt: F. KIDMAN.

To:- The Members of Auxiliary Units - Operational Branch.

The War Office has ordered that the Operational side of Auxiliary Units shall stand down! This is due to the greatly improved War situation and the strategic requirements of the moment.

I realize what joining Auxiliary Units has meant to you, so do the officers under my command. You were invited to do a job which would require more skill and coolness, more hard work and greater danger, than was demanded of any other voluntary organisation. In the event of "Action Stations" being ordered you knew well the kind of life you were in for. But that was in order; you were picked men; and others, including myself, knew that you would continue to fight whatever the conditions, with, or if necessary without, orders.

It now falls to me to tell you that your work has been appreciated and well carried out, and that your contract, for the moment, is at an end. I am grateful to you for the way you have trained in the last four years. So is the Regular Army. It was due to you that more divisions left this country to fight the battle of France; and it was due to your reputation for skill and determination that extra risk was taken - successfully as it turned out - in the defence arrangements of this country during that vital period. I congratulate you on this reputation and thank you for this voluntary effort.

In view of the fact that your lives depended on secrecy no public recognition will be possible. But those in the most responsible positions at General Headquarters, Home Forces, know what was done; and what would have been done had you been called upon. They know it well, as is emphasized in the attached letter from the Commander-in-Chief. It will not be forgotten.

Typewritten letter addressed to Sgt F Kidman, leader of North Walsham patrol. It is signed by Colonel FWR Douglas and dates from 18 November 1944.

Although the patrols were maintained in a state of readiness until they were stood down, some of their stores had gradually been called in as the threat of invasion receded. The remaining arms, ammunition, explosives, uniforms and rum rations were to be returned at stand-down but not all the stores issued over the years were actually collected. Auxiliary Units explosives, for instance, were used to fell trees or to blow up disused farm buildings for many years to come. Royal Engineers sappers were sent out to find and destroy or to make inaccessible by other means the patrols' operational bases that were scattered all over the county, but many OBs were far too well camouflaged and hence never found. Over the years, the odd one was discovered by children playing in the woods, and consequently removed or made inaccessible by landowners or by Community Council workers because of health and safety concerns. A surprisingly large number of operational bases, however, have quietly survived for decades - a long time, considering that they were never meant to last that long, especially so since Auxiliary Units patrol members were estimated to have a life expectancy of only a couple of weeks in the event of an invasion.

After stand-down on 1 November 1944, the auxiliers returned to their everyday lives. Many had already been called up to regular Army service or were encouraged to join Special Forces such as the Commandos, SAS (Special Air Service) or SIS (Secret Intelligence Service). The SAS - together with the Special Boat Service (SBS), Special Reconnaissance Regiment (SRR), and the Special Forces Support Group (SFSG) - form the UKSF (United Kingdom Special Forces), commanded by the Director Special Forces. Commando units comprised soldiers who had volunteered for Special Forces. As a raiding force, they used standard Army small arms including Lee-Enfield rifles, Bren, Sten and Thompson submachine guns, Webley revolvers and Colt .45 pistols. They were also issued the Fairbairn-Sykes fighting knife, which had been especially designed for use in hand-to-hand combat. Some of the auxiliers signed up with GHQ Liaison Regiment (Phantom), a special reconnaissance unit formed in 1939 and based at Pembroke Lodge in Richmond Park, London. Phantom was disbanded in 1945 but continued to operate as the Army Phantom Signals Regiment until 1960.

Most of the men never spoke about their activities in the Auxiliary Units, not even to close family. Their stand-down message arrived in form of a standard typewritten letter, signed by Col FWR Douglas and distributed to each one of the auxiliers:

> "The War Office has ordered that the Operational side of Auxiliary Units shall stand down! I realise what joining Auxiliary Units has meant to you; so do the officers under my command. You were invited to do a job which would require more skill and coolness, more hard work and greater danger, than was demanded of any other voluntary organisation ... It now falls to me to tell you that your work has been appreciated and well carried out, and that your contract, for the moment, is at an end. I am grateful for the way you have trained in the last four years. So is the Regular Army. It was due to you that more divisions left this country to fight the battle of France. ... In view of the fact that your lives depended on secrecy no public recognition will be possible.

Auxiliers were advised that they were not eligible for the Defence Medal because no written records of service had purportedly been kept. Subsequent events have shown this statement to be false and belated awards have since been made to at least some of the men involved. The great majority of auxiliers, however, have never received any public recognition, and the British Government and MOD have never issued a specific badge and/or letter of commendation to acknowledge their high level of training and commitment. Today, many people are still unaware of the fact that AU members (Ops

Branch only) who served for more than three years are entitled to a Defence Medal, and that relatives of auxiliers can apply for this medal on their behalf.

Several weeks after stand-down, the Auxiliers were presented a small red and blue metal lapel badge *(left)* by a local area IO. This is believed to have been arranged by MI6 but no records have to-date been found which would prove this. The lapel badge is often the only physical evidence that they have of their involvement with Auxiliary Units.

The Special Duties Branch (SD)

HQ SD was established on 22 July 1940, three weeks after HQ GHQ Aux Units. According to the Army Establishment notes, it already existed but was attached to AU on that date. The original HQ consisted of 27 all ranks, two staff officers, 11 IOs (each with his own 4-seater car and driver) and a couple of clerks. Signallers had as yet to be taken on board. Six months later (War Establishment dated 20 Feb 1941), the SD Branch included from Royal Signals an instrument mechanic and four Operator Wireless and Line (OWLs). Two OWLs were included in HQ AU and one OWL was attached to each of the Scout Sections. All OWLs came from the Royal Corps of Signals (RCS). There is also a note according to which "the following additional Royal Signals personnel will be allowed for the Special Duties Branch to be filled as and when required: Maj x 1; Capt x 1; Lt x 2; Sgt x 1; Cpl x 2, L/Cpl x 15; Signalmen x 26; Drvs (RASC) x 6; ATS x 40. The latter were soon to be tasked with setting up the secret wireless network, with the signallers being referred to as "Auxiliary Units Signals" and the ATS staff as "Auxiliary Units ATS". Capt Ken Ward has said that when he was posted to form part of a new unit, in January 1941, the unit's name was Auxiliary Units Signals.

The wireless network set up by the Special Duties Branch comprised people of all walks of life. Some were officers and signallers, referred to as Auxiliary Units (Signals). ATS officers manned many of the IN-Stations, whereas all the OUT-Stations - some of the AU signallers referred to them as "Coast Stations" because they were commonly situated much closer to the coast than the IN-Stations - were operated by civilians, frequently from their homes. It is believed that the OUT-Station operator would also have been the Key Man of his local network, i.e. he would have set up his own network of observers, allocated specific jobs and vetted his spies' reports before passing them on to the IN-Station – without his observers being aware of his real task. A number of OUT-Stations were dugouts in the woods, some were tucked away in the cellars or lofts of private houses or in farm sheds, whilst others were kept hidden in pubs or even in churches, under the altar or pulpit, or up in the belfry. All the civilian wireless operators as well as their helpers, the observers, had of course been first vetted for their suitability. The observers deposited information to be picked up by runners or couriers, who in turn passed on this information to their OUT-Station. There it would have been coded and transmitted to the local IN-Station, and passed on to the Intelligence branch at the Army HQ responsible for that area.

During the four years of the organisation's existence, by 1944, altogether 30 IN-Stations (also referred to as Control Stations, as they controlled the secret wireless traffic within their area network), 125 OUT-Stations and 78 SUB-OUT-Stations had been constructed and equipped with wireless sets and aerials. All stations were sited at strategic locations in coastal areas (with the OUT-Stations situated nearer to the coast than the IN-Stations), ranging from the East coast of Scotland, to Northumberland, Lincolnshire and East Anglia and along the south coast to East Devon, with some along the South Wales coast. The number of civilians involved in this spy network amounted to at least 3,250 men and women, who had been trained to gather information, to identify vehicles, high-ranking officers and military units, and to leave their reports in dead letter drops where runners would collect them.

The following brief description comes from an official report, authored by Maj RMA Jones, Officer Commanding of Auxiliary Units Signals, in 1944. The report contains a summary of the task of IN-Stations. Maj Jones' report survives in the National Archives. *(See also Appendices H and I)*

> "The Special Duties Branch of Auxiliary Units is organised to provide information for military formations in the event of enemy invasion or raids in Great Britain, from areas temporarily or permanently in enemy control. All this information would be collected as a result of direct observation by specially recruited and trained civilians who would remain in an enemy occupied area. Auxiliary Units Signals are responsible for providing the communications to enable the civilian observers to pass their information to a military HQ. All traffic is by wireless (R/T), using very high frequency sets. Information is collected at IN-Stations (manned by Royal Signals or ATS officers) and is passed from there to mil fmn *(military formation)*. IN-Stations have concealed dugouts in which station crew can, if necessary, live without coming above ground at all for three weeks at a time. This includes provision for battery charging, feeding etc." *(TNA reference: WO.199/1194)*

Initially there were no wireless communications and one might assume that runners would have had to cross the 'front line' to deliver their reports. In 1941, AU Signals were formed to take responsibility for providing the communications to enable the civilian observers to pass the information to a military HQ by wireless (radio/telephony). Throughout the coastal areas which were likely to be invaded, over 200 concealed wireless stations manned entirely by civilians were set up. It has been documented that IN-Stations conducted their everyday wireless traffic from huts and that, from 1942 onwards, concealed dugouts that contained provisions for 21 days were built near the majority of these huts. Crews could, if necessary, live in their dugout without coming above ground at all for three weeks at a time. This included the provision of battery charging, feeding and toilet facilities. The IN-Stations were staffed by either AU Signals or by ATS officers, the OUT and SUB-OUT-Stations entirely by civilians. Maj Jones produced a map of the whole network in July 1944 that shows the approximate locations of IN-Stations and the links to and the locations of their OUT-Stations, as they existed in 1944. This is about the extent of information that is available from original contemporary sources, which have only been released in more recent years. Although now declassified, many questions remain as yet unresolved.

The team at Bachelor's Hall, Hundon

In early 1941, Capt (later Maj) Hills, assisted by Capt Ken Ward, and his team started to recruit radio "hams" who were given the task of designing and manufacturing a small radio telephony set that would be simple to use and could withstand damp conditions. They were based at Bachelor's Hall at Hundon (South Suffolk). When Maj Hills left

AU Signals, Maj RMA Jones, who used to work at Pye Radio before he came into the Army, replaced him. Maj Green commanded the unit at stand-down.

The first headquarters of Auxiliary Units Signals were set up at a fine manorial house located on the outskirts of the village of Hundon in South Suffolk. Bachelor's Hall is set back from the road and surrounded by a large garden, which at the time also had an orchard. A number of outbuildings, a large barn amongst them, adjoin the house which is now a family home. Capt Ken Ward says that Maj John Hills met him around Christmas 1940, and asked if he would be interested to join a new project as his staff captain, adjutant and workshop officer. The major pointed out that the men should bring along their wives because female wireless operators were required. Thea Ward was one of the first wireless operators at Halstead (Essex) IN-Station.

It did not take long for the posting order directing Capt Ward to report to Maj John Hills at The Bull public house in Long Melford to arrive. He not only found Maj Hills with his wife and two children already living at the Bull, but there were also Capt Freddie Childe (the IO) as well as Cpls Chalk and Crawley, both RASC. Capt Ward recalls:

> "So I arrived at Long Melford. John was living in the Bull with his wife and two kids and Freddie Childe, who was the IO, was living there as well.... anyway, so I was taken upstairs to a bedroom which they had converted into an office and Freddie Childe read the riot act to me and made me swear to the Official Secrets Act."

Soon it was decided to find a suitable location in East Anglia:

> "Because that was the next area to be dealt with and it was fairly central to the whole of the coast. So we scoured around and we eventually discovered that Bachelor's Hall had been vacated by the Manchester Regiment, who had been accommodated there, and was empty. So we went and had a look at it and decided that it had what we needed. Well it hadn't got electricity, but you had a big house here with hot and cold water, oil lamps, Tilley lanterns, you know, and a range of outbuildings... at the back there was a large farmhouse kitchen which was capable of feeding the troops and plumbing, two septic tanks and that sort of thing with main drainage. At the back there was a large barn, which was ideal for working." *(Capt Ward)*.

Initially, the unit consisted only of a handful of men: Tom Higgins and Ron Dabbs designed the receiver, Bill Bartholomew and Jack Millie the transmitter; Les Parnell, Jimmy McNab and John Mackie were in charge of designing the power supply and metalwork, with Bill Air completing the team. One man (George Spencer) was allocated the task of choosing suitable IN-Station sites, which, for obvious reasons, needed to be concealed from the public. Suitable trees for the erection of aerials and providing good wireless reception also needed to be found in the vicinity. All the stations required copper-wire dipole aerials. Where possible, the aerials were strung in high trees, with the aerial feeder cables being hidden in V-shaped grooves that had been cut out of the tree bark. After placing the copper wire in the groove it was covered by the previously removed strip of bark. The normal working range of the sets was up to about 30 miles but the longest range achieved was 64 miles (100 kilometres). The team was under the command of Capt Shanks. AU Signals eventually numbered 69 men. For administrative purposes they were attached to a unit at nearby Clare where there also was a ration stand from which they drew their rations.

Bachelor's Hall in 2012

After Bachelor's Hall had been chosen and approved of, personnel and transport had to also be found.

> "So we went beating around the bush with not much success and the first thing that we got was a bunch of RASC drivers, I think there were about nine of them, and they had been in the Army for a week, so they weren't exactly military but they were all trained drivers, except one who was a chap from Glasgow, and he came into the office and I said 'have you got a clean driving licence?' They had all got clean driving licenses, and he said, yes, he had a clean license. 'Can you manage a Ford V8 Staff Car?' He said 'I don't know sir, I've never driven a car, I was 2nd hand on a steam wagon'. He was a great bloke."

Asked if there was one set of IOs for the Auxiliary Units patrols and another for the spy networks, Capt Ward said that he didn't know. All he knew was that Capt Fred Childe was the IO for East Anglia, Capt Fleming in the South, Capt Owen Hall-Hall down in Dorset and Maj John Collings in Norfolk.

Unlike AU operational patrols and Scout Sections, who knew of each others' existence and often worked together, the men and women of Special Duties Branch, be they Army or civilian, had no contact with the operations branch, which in turn, at least officially, knew about the existence of a secret wireless network operating in their areas only at the highest level on a need to know basis. Intelligence Officers would have had a need to know and hence would have been aware, although perhaps not fully informed, about Special Duties Branch operations in their respective counties. There are some indications, however that at least some of the AU patrols operating near a wireless station did know about its existence, albeit purely through observation.

157

One of the AU Signals officers was sent out to liase with the AU operational patrols' IOs, acting as the only link between the two. Capt Ward thought that although there was this tenuous link, they never *officially* knew that the AU operational patrols existed. At that time his team was not manufacturing sets for the AU patrols. Asked if he knew anything about AU patrols having been issued with standard domestic Murphy's receivers in 1943, and which purpose these might have served, Capt Ward replied: "Probably for socialising to stop the guys getting bored, I can't think of any other reason."

Capt Ward confirmed that all the sets they built were to be used at civilian locations, by civilians who would remain in enemy occupied territory.

> "Farmers, vicars, bakers, butchers, candlestick makers, bar maids, all sorts of strange people and each of them had a wireless station somewhere near the coast where they could know what was happening. And they had a network of reporters working to them, people just wandering around the countryside who had put a message in a tennis ball and roll it down a chute into the station or whatever."

The transport used for maintaining the OUT-Stations were often old motorcycles with sidecars, of which they had 24.

> "So 24 motorbikes arrived with another bunch of men, who had to be trained to ride motorbikes with side cars on them, well it's one thing riding a motorbike without a side car but it's quite a different thing, we made an awful mess of the fences and ditches around Hundon, most of them succeeded in the end. So these teams of 2 would go out from wherever they were based and visit the stations, change the batteries, charge the batteries, they were responsible for battery charging at the 'met' huts, normally they worked from a 'met' hut out to the area, but they had to be very careful not to be seen when they went near to the station and that sort of thing. In some areas we actually sent them in civilian vehicles. So that was all part of the Hundon operation."

According to Ken Ward, the men set up altogether 480 working stations over the period of one year at Bachelor's Hall. Once a network was fully operational the stations were taken over by permanent operators. At first Savage sets were used, so called because they were built by Brian Savage Ltd. At some stage, however, the men were getting increasingly frustrated with these sets, which according to Capt Ward were difficult to open, difficult to repair and not very well built. Consequently, they decided to develop their own and within about three weeks, says Ken Ward, they had produced what became known as the TRD. A reproduction version of a TRD as it might have looked can be seen on display at the British Resistance Organisation Museum at Parham (Suffolk). All attempts to re-create a fully operational TRD set have to-date failed. Capt Ward and his team not only built the sets and installed them in the coast stations *(OUT-Stations run by civilians)* they also instructed the operators on how to use them. They had their own test station at Bachelor's Hall, housed in one of the upstairs bedrooms, where all their sets were tested working to 'Buttercup', the IN-Station at Halstead (Essex). The operators at 'Buttercup' were Mickey Brown and Thea Ward *(Capt Ken Ward's wife)*.

The equipment used by the summer of 1944 in the various IN, OUT and SUB-OUT-Stations consisted of 250 TRD sets, specially built either in the HQ workshop or by contract; 28 TRM sets, 36 TRF sets and 200 No 17 sets and the frequencies allotted ranged between 48 – 65 mcs *(megacycles/second)*. TRDs used 6 volt, 85 AH accumulators. The transmitter was set on a fixed frequency which, except for minor adjustments, could be changed only in workshops. Different sets were used for handset and loudspeaker use. The latter appear to have been used in IN-Stations. The transmitter power output was approximately 1½ watt. The controls consisted of an on/off switch, a send/receive switch, a receiver tuning dial and a volume control knob. The transmitter had a speech amplifier, modulator and push-pull oscillator; the receiver comprised an RF stage, super regenerative detector and an output stage. *(Major Jones report, National Archives)*

Lady 'Biddy' Carlisle and Senior Commander Beatrice Temple, ATS

ATS cap badge

A.T.S.: South-Eastern Command Officers
Chief Commandant the Countess of Carlisle (right) is Assistant Director, A.T.S., South-Eastern Command. On the staff is Company Commander Cynthia Charrington, daughter of Brigadier Charrington

(Photo source and date unknown)

Parallel with the building of wireless sets and IN-Stations, operators were required and, presumably to save military manpower, it was decided that these should be recruited from the ATS. The first ATS officers were recruited by Chief Controller of ATS, Lady Bridget Helen "Biddy" Monckton, otherwise known as the Countess of Carlisle. After passing two training courses, one held at No.1 ATS OCTU at Craigmillar in Edinburgh, the first five ATS wireless operators soon started working at an IN-Station in Kent which formed part of the original pilot scheme.

Asked if the pay books of the signallers that were posted in were stamped "Auxiliary Units (Signals)", Capt Ward said "Oh yes, we were called that before we existed and it is what I was posted to". ATS and AU signallers were accommodated, with board, in civilian billets which had been arranged by the local police. For administrative purposes they were attached to the nearest area headquarters but ATS depended on Royal Corps of Signals for transport as well as for technical assistance.

> "In view of the highly specialised nature of the wireless set and the most secret nature of their task, it is strongly recommended that personnel be carefully selected with an officer of the AU Signals branch taking part at the interview. Only men of responsible character and discretion should be entertained. Their medical category however need not be high except that their speech and hearing must be of standard suited for R/T transmission."
> (Memorandum dated April 1942)

When Beatrice Temple (1907 - 1982), the niece of William Temple (the then Archbishop of Canterbury) was commissioned as a 2nd subaltern on 30 May 1941, she had already served several years with ATS. She was appointed Senior Commander in May 1942. According to a long-term friend "she liked to organise things".

Beatrice Temple grew up in India where her father was a District Engineer. Living with a friend in Elgin (Scotland) at the time, Beatrice Temple volunteered for service in the Auxiliary Territorial Service (ATS) in September 1938. She had initially wanted to join the Women's Royal Naval Service (WRNS) because she wanted to stay in Scotland and be able to travel about. She wanted to drive lorries too, but seemingly she never did. Instead, in 1938, she volunteered for service in the ATS, recalling later that she would have volunteered for any organisation that wouldn't tell her beforehand what it was all about. At around the same time she must have also done some training with the British Red Cross because her exercise book, containing notes on emergency cooking and food supply, morale and the establishment of rest centres is listed in the inventory of the Imperial War Museum.

Only eight women enrolled on that day together with Beatrice Temple, five of them as cooks. The authorities thought that Miss Temple would be more suitable for doing paperwork and she was promoted to captain almost straight away, and given the job of ATS company commander, attached to the Seaforth Highlanders. "I had only five days to become an officer. I learned to drill with sergeants in the Guards and studied military law but my job consisted mainly of doing administrative work." On receiving her movement order at the outbreak of war, Miss Temple nearly got herself into deep trouble when promoting many sergeants and corporals without first obtaining permission from the War Office. Two months later the paymaster pointed out that she had no authority to promote them, but fortunately all promotions were later confirmed. According to some accounts, the instructions issued to those who were to undergo selection as ATS wireless operators and sent to take a voice test at Bachelor's Hall required that they take a train from Liverpool Street station, change at Marks Tey and get out at Hundon, from where they were to make their way to the 'Rose and Crown' public house where a car would come for them. Hundon, however, never had a railway station - the nearest stations would have been at Clare or Haverhill. Capt Ken Ward recalled that the candidates were commonly picked up from Colchester station.

Beatrice Temple is said to have interviewed about 100 women and, after passing their voice tests, 43 candidates are believed to have finally been chosen for training. The May 1942 Establishment however shows that the number of AU ATS at that time amounted to 104. After commissioning as 2nd subalterns they were allocated to an IN-Station in groups of three per station.

In 1942, AU Signals HQ moved from Hundon to Hannington Hall near Highworth in

Wiltshire. The War Establishment (dated 30 May 1942) shows a significant increase in the numbers of Royal Signals OWLs, whereas the numbers of ATS were reduced from 104 to 31. Of interest is a note mentioning, for the first time, a Senior Commander ATS *(Beatrice Temple)*, a clerk, a driver and a 4-seater car *(all in AU HQ)*.

The 17th century Hall, at the time owned by the Fry family, the Quakers and chocolate makers, provided staff accommodation and a number of offices which were used for administrative purposes. A small administrative staff and a workshop, where major repairs and special work was carried out, were located in the grounds of Coleshill House. Barbara M Culleton (personal number 205716) recalls that she worked both at Hannington Hall and at Coleshill House, which was only a couple of miles distant.

Group photo of the ATS Team taken at Hannington Hall

Front row from left to right: Lady "Biddy" Carlisle, Beatrice Temple and Barbara Culleton
(Photo source: J Winterborn)

Miss Culleton appears to have been one of the subalterns affected by the aforementioned cull in ATS numbers: her military service record shows that she was posted to Combined Operations at the beginning of May 1942, at the same time that Beatrice Temple was appointed AU ATS Group Commander. In the autumn of 1941, Barbara Culleton had spent some time at Hickleton Hall in the West Riding district of Yorkshire, where the IN-Station was housed in a gazebo situated in the extensive gardens:

> "I well remember the adjutant, suitably booted and spurred, riding to work each morning."

Asked about the term "Secret Sweeties", which had been attributed to the ATS wireless operators by David Lampe in his book *(The Last Ditch)*, Barbara Culleton remarks that this label was unheard of during her time with the organisation.

After closedown *(the SD equivalent of stand-down)*, Beatrice Temple spent the rest of the war in unexciting jobs in ATS administration where she finally reached the rank of chief commander, the equivalent of lieutenant colonel. For some time she also served as Mayor of Lewes, Sussex, where she lived. Sadly, the diary she had kept during her time with AU ATS was later destroyed. Only a few snippets and short notes have survived.

The local wireless networks

Special Duties Branch IO for Norfolk was Major John Collings (of the elite 5th Royal Inniskilling Dragoon Guards), who was replaced in the spring of 1944, by Capt Douglas Ingrams RA, the SD IO from Taunton, Somerset, who took over. Lt Frederick Childe was IO for Suffolk and Essex. Because East Anglia is mainly flat terrain, the IN-Stations could sometimes be sited no higher than their OUT-Stations and it is for this reason that some of the IN-Stations here are situated much closer to each other than anywhere else.

Once arrived at an IN-Station, any information was passed on to the nearest Intelligence branch at the Army HQ responsible for that area (commonly located in the immediate vicinity). There, additional information, originating from a number of other sources, would of course also be gathered. The combined information was then sent to the Command HQ (in East Anglia this was Eastern Command, based at Horse Guards Parade, London, and later at Luton Hoo, Bedfordshire) in the form of Intelligence Summaries (INTSUMs). Combined with Intelligence gathered by the Command HQs' own sources, the total of information concerning the area of responsibility, including the information gathered by SD Branch, was passed on to GS Int at GHQ HF as the final destination for all Intelligence. In his stand-down letter (dated 4 July 1944) General Sir Harold E Franklyn, Commander in Chief of GHQ Home Forces, writes: "The security reports regularly provided by Special Duties have proved of invaluable assistance to our security staffs." (*See also Appendix H*)

The first IN-Stations were commonly small huts and that was just as well, as Commander Temple admitted that "for fear of claustrophobia, I should not have cared to crawl along the long escape tunnels (in dugouts), however how many Germans would have been after me". The huts were furnished to look like Meteorological huts, with barometric charts on the walls and other relevant paraphernalia on display. It has been documented that at least some were supplied with a daily weather forecast *(Ken Ward)*. In the early days the huts were located at or in close vicinity to an Army HQ. Not only would these locations have been well protected but also the passing on of information from IN-Station to an officer in the G Intelligence Staff would have been quick and immediate. Each hut contained two (sometimes three) wireless sets, operated in shifts by between three and five ATS operators. A simple code was used for reports coming in from their OUT-Stations. Contrary to some reports, Morse code was never used. Most 'met' huts appear to have been dismantled after the war. As none of them seems to have survived, and because details regarding their construction and interior are, for obvious reasons, scarce and based entirely on recollections, and sometimes on hearsay, all information relating to their design ought to be taken with a pinch of salt.

There is some evidence to support the theory that IN-Station dugouts, the construction of which started sometime in mid-1942, were sited some distance away from the HQ and it follows that the huts might consequently have been moved as well. The dugouts were constructed to give better protection for the stay-behind IN-Station operators in the event of enemy troops occupying the area the station was located in. The huts continued to serve for everyday use but they had to be situated close enough to a dugout so that the latter could be reached quickly, on foot, in an emergency. For reasons as yet to be fully understood, a small number of IN-Station huts appear to have remained at their original locations until closedown in 1944, and some never seemed to have had a dugout. The IN-Station dugouts were sometimes referred to as 'Zero' Stations, so-called because, according to David Lampe *(The Last Ditch)*, whenever the operators transmitted from them they followed the station's name with the code suffix 'zero'. Little evidence has been found that this would indeed have been the case, and a specific suffix would certainly not have been required to differentiate between operation from the "Met" hut and the dugout. Barbara Culleton does not recall the use of the term. Interestingly, though, Sergeant Alf Ellis (AU Signals) in his 1942 diary refers to a newly constructed dugout site as 'Zero'. Built by Royal Engineers who were unaware of their intended use, the dugouts consisted of an entrance chamber that was accessed through a vertical shaft. A concealed door led from the antechamber or lobby at the foot of the shaft into the wireless room which had another door at its far end, giving access to an adjoining room which housed the generator required for the recharging of batteries. There was also an emergency escape exit, commonly extending to some distance away from the structure. Most dugouts were built to the same design. Roy Russell, AU Signals officer in charge of two IN-Stations in Kent, gives a detailed account of how they were designed:

"A Royal Engineer officer came and took us to our two units. They had been built ready for our occupation. I did not see the stations being built, but when they were operating I went in a lot and I remember well what they were like. To get into the underground station you had to crank a shaft. You knew more or less where the entrance was and you had to find a particularly small flat stone. You moved that, and underneath you could see where the crank fitted. You could turn that, and up came a piece of grass which was like a manhole cover, covered with turf so no join could be seen. When it came up, it revealed a shaft and at a certain height you could swing it away and climb underneath it. You then used the crankshaft to reseal it. The shaft was 4-sided and about the size of a trap door and it was wood-lined. There was no ladder but wooden steps, fastened to one side. You climbed down about eight feet, on to a concrete floor.

The structure was a Nissen hut, but with corrugated iron arched across to form a roof. At the bottom *(of the shaft)* there was a room, about six by nine feet, with shelving all around, and on one shelf there was an empty shell magazine, which gave the impression that the place was an empty ammunition dump. On one of the shelves lay a piece of wire. If you knew what to look for, there was a small hole in the woodwork into which you could push the wire. Something activated the other side, and the whole of that side cantilevered. If you bent down you could walk in and close it behind you. You were now in a room where you would see two tables with wireless sets and three ATS officers operating them. Beyond the "Set" room there was a room with cooking facilities, and Elsans, and there was a room for battery charging. Everything was powered by batteries which had to be recharged by a little engine – a "Chorehorse" – petrol driven – in a tubular cage. The exhaust from that was led away by a duct and came out some way away, where you could only just hear it. The last room led to an emergency exit plus tunnel which was a heavy duty concrete culvert pipe measuring 30 inches in diameter."

Royal Corps of Signals cap badge *(left)*. The GHQ Home Forces formation badge *(right)* was worn on both sleeves under the regimental shoulder titles by all ranks of Royal Signals serving in the HQ or in units directly under the HQ.

At stand-down *(see Appendices B and I)* the huts were cleared of furniture and dismantled. The concrete platforms on which some of the huts stood can occasionally still be found. The dugouts too were stripped of all furniture and their exit and entrance openings were capped with thick layers of reinforced concrete. The aerials are long gone but with some luck the odd feeder cable running up a tree has remained in situ, although frequently quite deteriorated after having been exposed to the elements for seven decades.

The cable commonly used as aerial feeder was known as 'BA 3 AP' cable and it has been documented that altogether 30,000 yards of it were ordered between August 1942 and May 1944 *(see page 201)*. It has as yet to be discovered exactly why such a large quantity of cable would have been required.

During the summer of 1944, all wireless sets were returned – WS17 and WS36 *(WS = wireless sets)* transmitters were sent to the depot at Woolwich and all 'special sets' (the TRDs, TRMs and TRFs) were taken to No. 1 SCU (Special Communications Unit) at Whaddon Hall, where extreme care apparently was taken to completely destroy them. Not even the smallest part of one appears to have survived. The AU signallers were returned to Catterick Camp in Yorkshire for Signals training to enable them to be posted to normal Signals units. The Signal Training Centre retained some as instructors. Most of the AU ATS officer wireless operators were discharged from the Army and moved on to civilian jobs and everybody else who had been involved had soon returned to their ordinary lives. Most never talked about their wartime activities and were it not for Ken Ward, Alf Ellis, Frank Hewitt, Les Parnell, Arthur Gabbitas and Roy Russell (AU Signals) and a handful of ATS subalterns (including Barbara Culleton, Yolande Bromley, Marina Bloxam and others but not Senior Commander Temple, so it seems), who many years later shared at least some of their experiences, next to nothing would today be known about the secret wireless networks of the AU Special Duties Branch.

Sgt Frank Hewitt and Sgt Roy Russell *(right)* of Auxiliary Units Signals
(Photo dates and sources unknown)

Codes

Much has been written and speculated regarding the secret code used for transmitting messages from OUT to IN-Stations. David Lampe, who was fortunate to have met Col (later Brigadier) Bill Major, is quite clear about the issue. He writes that a friend of Col Major invented a code sheet that consisted of 500-odd military words and phrases. A single letter code matched these phrases and arrangements were made to change the code on a daily basis *(The Last Ditch, p 134)*.

Sgt Stanley Judson - he joined AU direct from the NCOs' Training Battalion in Harrogate and was posted to Sudbury (Bachelor's Hall, Hundon, Suffolk) and, together with his team of signallers helped to set up the wireless networks in Lincolnshire, Yorkshire and Norfolk – in a letter to his former colleague, A Gabbitas, dated 11 Feb 1995 *(in BROM Archive)*, recalls:

> "I remember the code quite well. It was a sheet, divided into squares or oblongs, and in each square there was an Army term and a different description so somebody could say "Able Y" and the person receiving the message would look on the code sheet and it would say "50 tanks", or whatever. All these sort of things were put in the different squares so you related the top with the side and the letters and that gave the clue to what the message was." *(J Warwicker, IWM 29468, 1999)*

In 1943-44 the Army introduced a hand-held, paper-based encoding system working on the same principle and it continued to be used up to well into the 1970s. Called "Slidex", it consisted of 204 boxes containing letters and words. The letters on the cursors were set each day in the daily Signals Instructions and the code was easy to use and well liked by troops. Its security, however, is said to have been illusory. The recollections of former ATS operators are less clear and often conflicting, although all are agreed that Morse code was never used. Janet Wise (nee Purves-Smith) believed that they had to eat the code sheets *(Stephen Sutton, IWM 14817, 11 Aug 1994)*. Marina Bloxam thought that their contact telephone numbers changed according to the code they were using.

> "We had a code which we knew the "key" to. We had it in our heads or waistcoat pocket." *(Stephen Sutton, IWM 14816, 31 Oct 1994)*

Jill Monk (nee Holman) recalls that her mother used to do the coding but she could not remember how often the code was changed and how it arrived at their OUT-Station. She thought the signaller who regularly called to change the batteries might have delivered it. Yolande Alston (nee Bromley) remembers that there was a code and that it changed daily but very little else:

> "Tanks and things were called 'cows' or 'bulls' so that if we'd been picked up it would be women having a silly chat about cows. I can't remember being given training in code work but we must have, we must have had the codes. We changed the code every day and then the sheet was thrown away or destroyed. I expect we had instructions but I can't remember any of that." *(J Warwicker, IWM 29457, 28 Feb 1997)*

Wynne Read, who worked at the Heathfield Park IN-Station in East Sussex, recalls that the codes for their messages were based on various unlikely texts, including some of the comic verses contributed to *Punch* by Patrick Barrington (later the 11th Viscount Barrington), one of which began:

> "I had a duck-billed platypus when I was up at Trinity
> For whom I developed a remarkable affinity.
> He used to live in lodgings with myself and Arthur Purvis,
> And we all went up together for the Diplomatic Service."

IN and OUT-Stations

SUB-OUT and OUT-Stations run by civilians sent information to their local networks'
IN-Station and the IN-Stations were linked with stations further inland, the so-called
Inner Network. The wireless networks in Norfolk and Suffolk comprised three IN-
Stations. One was near Norwich, Norfolk, one near Thornham Magna, a village in Mid-
Suffolk district and a third in the Hardwick area of Bury St Edmunds. The Norfolk
network (call-sign Bowling) had links to seven and the Suffolk network (call-sign
Chariot) to five OUT-Stations. The Hardwick site was linked with Thornham Magna.
SUB-OUT-Stations are not marked on Major Jones' map and hence their exact number
remains unknown. Both the Norfolk and Suffolk IN-Stations were linked with a station
on the Inner Network (call-sign Gorey), located near the village of Ousden (in Suffolk's
St Edmundsbury district). This station did not have OUT-Stations. The two links
extending from it in south-westerly direction lead to the Essex IN-Station near Halstead
(Buttercup) and to an as yet unidentified Inner Network station in Hertfordshire.

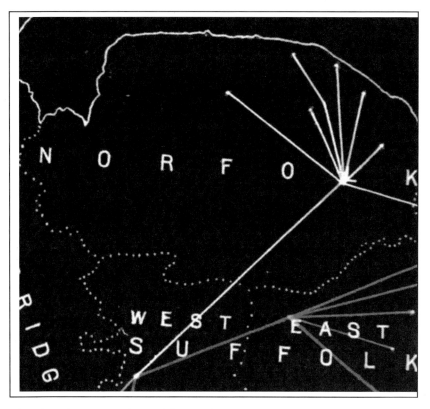

A small section of Major Jones' map. *(The complete original map, which is in colour, can be seen
at the National Archives.)*

As can be seen in the above map section showing the Norfolk and Suffolk wireless
networks, the IN-Stations were located further inland from their OUT-Stations. The dot
below the 'S' of Suffolk, where four lines (links) meet, marks the location of the south-
easternmost station on the Inner Network, near the village of Ousden *(see page 169)*.
No OUT-Stations are associated with it.

Thornham Magna IN-Station

Call sign: Chariot

Thornham Magna and its twin village Thornham Parva, about a mile distant, are situated in Mid Suffolk, nestling in a rural countryside traversed by the gently meandering River Dove. The Henniker family of Thornham Magna Hall historically owned most of the surrounding land.

During the war, Thornham Park was the HQ of 15th (Scottish) Division and the IN-Station was housed in a 'Met' hut located within the confines of the military camp. According to one of the wireless operators, Yolande Bromley, the hut had a toilet and cooking and rest facilities, and it was connected to mains electricity which was apparently used for charging the batteries. The AU signallers assigned to 15th Division were stationed in Eye, about four miles distant, whereas the ATS operators were billeted in the Red House, the home of the Hon John Henniker, Lord Henniker's youngest brother, and his wife Molly. The station's two main wireless operators were Yolande Bromley (married name: Alston) and Margaret Whiting, both ATS.

The IN-Station was linked to a network of OUT-Stations. Both available maps – one dated 1944, by Major Jones, Officer Commanding of Auxiliary Units Signals, the other created in about 1995 from recollections by Corporal Arthur Gabbitas and some of his former of AU Signals colleagues – are agreed on there having been five OUT-Stations. Two of these stations are mentioned briefly *(in Sergeant Alf Ellis' 1942 diary)* - Uggeshall (call-sign Chariot 3) and Peasenhall (call-sign Chariot 2). Information received at Thornham Magna IN-Station was passed on to the nearby Divisional HQ. An IN-Station in the Hardwick area on the southern fringe of Bury St Edmunds, was added to the network in the autumn of 1942. Thornham Magna IN-Station was linked with Ousden Control Station, a station on the Inner Network, which also had links to Halstead IN-Station (Buttercup) in Essex and to Norwich IN-Station (Bowling) - two of the first three IN-Stations that were built in East Anglia.

Beatrice Temple visited the Thornham Magna site on a regular basis while it was run by ATS. She made altogether six visits, the first on 15 Dec 1941, noting that she met Margaret Whiting and Yolande Bromley at the hut; on 1 April 1942 she spoke to Yolande Bromley and Kitty Hills (wife of Major Hills); on 7 May 1942 she met Capt FD Oakey (who later assisted Major RMA Jones, Royal Signals, OC AU Signals); on 10 July 1942 the operators' names are given as Seaver and Clifford. The final entry for Thornham Magna was made on 6 Oct 1942. It reads: "last time – Airlie alone".

Yolande Bromley (205953), who was commissioned as a 2nd subaltern on 20 July 1941, remembers barometric charts and other weather data on the walls of their hut and also that they did not have a dugout: "I have never been down one of these dugouts because there wasn't one at Thornham" and: "Our aerial was not on the hut's roof but up a tree. It was not on the tree we were underneath, as far as I remember, it was a bit, well, there was a little group of trees." The ATS stayed at Thornham Magna until October 1942, after which time the IN-Station hut was moved out of the park and into a nearby private wood, situated further to the east. The reason for the move appears to have been the establishment of a prisoner of war camp within the park, in autumn 1942. The Italian, and later German prisoners lived in huts in the old garden and in the woods *("Painful Extractions", Lord John Henniker, 2002)*. The ATS were consequently moved to a new location, where Waddy Cole (230660), who had previously worked at Norwich IN-Station, joined them.

In a letter *(to J Warwicker, dated 22 Feb 1997)* Yolande Bromley states that the new IN-Station was located in the Hardwick area of Bury St Edmunds. There the MoD

had requisitioned a former flax factory site, at the time occupied by the Bury Hand Laundry. The buildings have since been demolished to make way for a new housing development. As the West Suffolk Sub-Area HQs (11th Corps) were based in Bury St Edmunds after September 1941, the IN-Station, which Yolande Bromley says she opened it, appears to have been a later addition to the local network that served the 11th Corps Sub-Area HQs. Other ATS wireless operators known to have worked at Hardwick are Mickey Brown and Mary Shaw. Three bicycles were delivered to them on 1 December 1942. Bury St Edmunds was considered a safe zone for evacuees, which probably explains why the IN-Station had no dugout. When the HQs moved, the site seems to have been abandoned again as it is not shown on the 1944 map drawn by Major Jones.

Probably the most convincing evidence that AU Signals continued running operations from the new location at Thornham Magna is the record of a fatal accident, which is documented to have occurred six months after ATS had left the site. One of the AU Signals maintenance men, Cpl Laurence Tee, climbed up an oak tree to check the aerial when the rope broke and he fell, landing on his back. He was taken to Ipswich hospital where he died. The accident is confirmed by Stanley Judson, one of the AU Signals NCOs in charge of servicing the wireless stations *(letter and taped interviews conducted by John Warwicker, BRO Museum, Parham, Suffolk)*. The date of Cpl Tee's death, on 16 April 1943, is carved into his gravestone. He was 30 years old and his grave can be found in the churchyard of St Michael's at Boldmere near Birmingham.

Scarred bark of an old oak tree in Paradise Wood, Thornham. Aerial feeder cables were frequently hidden in groves cut out of a tree's bark. The bark was then replaced to cover the cable but over the years the scars became visible. However, tree scars can have natural causes such as lightning strike.

Ousden IN-Station (Inner Network)

Call sign: Gorey

Besides the majority of IN-Stations, which all received information from a number of local OUT-Stations, there were other stations, located further inland, to which they were linked. The latter formed part of the so-called Inner Network. According to Maj Jones, most of these stations served the Command HQs which were commonly situated relatively far inland. Characteristically, none of this type of stations had OUT-Stations of their own. Ousden was one of only three stations which handled transmissions from three networks, each of which working on a different frequency (65, 60 and 52 mcs respectively). As TRDs were set to a specific frequency that could only be changed in a workshop, one wireless set per frequency, each with its own aerial, would have been required (unless the versions referred to as TRF and TRM were tuneable).

Ousden is a small village in West Suffolk, situated about 12 kilometres south-west of Bury St Edmunds and 10 kilometres east of Newmarket near the Suffolk – Cambridgeshire border. Ousden is only about five kilometres distant from Batchelor's Hall in the village of Hundon, Suffolk. The nearest Army headquarters - 2 Corps HQ - were at Lower Hare Park near Newmarket, about 15 kilometres distant. Les Parnell, one of the AU Signals officers based in the area, confirms that from the station at Ousden information was passed on to 2 Corps by telephone *(letter to Dr W Ward, dated 28 March 1999).*

From an eyewitness report *(Mr Ted Knights)* it is known that the operators worked in a wooden hut. It stood in the north-eastern corner of Littly Wood *(currently owned by the Wills Charitable Trust),* not far from the edge and near the small village cemetery. The hut was situated on high ground at approximately 130 metres above sea level, almost as high as anybody can get in Suffolk. Capt Ken Ward remembers that the ATS operators based at Ousden were supplied with a daily weather forecast as a cover story in case somebody asked. A small shed housing the generator stood at one corner. It has been established that the wireless links between Ousden and Thorpe St Andrew/Norwich, to Halstead, and to Thornham Magna were all line-of-sight wireless paths. *(Source: Brian Drury)*

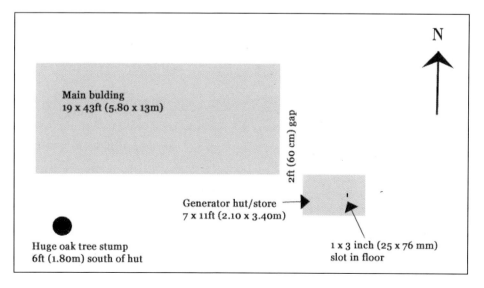

The following information originates from an interview with Mr Ted Knights, conducted by Dr William Ward (CART) in 1999. Mr Knights lived in the house adjoining the small cemetery situated near the IN-Station. The ATS subalterns (billeted at Dalham Hall, three kilometres away as the crow flies) stored their bicycles in the disused washhouse in Mr Knights' garden.

> "Commonly two of them would arrive in the morning and stay all day, to be replaced by two others at night. During times of heavy troop movements (exercises) altogether five of them would arrive. Occasionally a man called round in order to deliver water."

Mr Knights recalls that the hut was built from wood and stood on a concrete base.

> "Soldiers had arrived in trucks and felled the absolute minimum of trees, leaving the remainder for cover. They then laid a concrete base and brought the materials required for building the hut in a couple of trucks." (See also diagram on page 169)

After completion, a few strands of barbed wire on stakes were set up to surround the compound. After the war, Mr Knights went into the hut. He described it as having been a large room with a few windows. It had a toilet and a stove and what he thought to have been a pitched roof. The hut was dismantled and the components removed by the Army after the war. The wood was felled in 1955 and replanted in 1966. Mr Knights was certain that there was no underground site – he used to walk most days in the woods and was sure that he would have found it.

Site of Ousden IN-Station, with the small concrete platform exposed *(in foreground)*.

Marina Bloxam - a volunteer from FANY – seems to be the only person involved who believed that there was a dugout at Ousden. Her description, however, does not conform to any of the known designs of IN-Station dugouts. Les Parnell remembers that the aerial was up a tree, with the feeder cable hidden in a groove that was cut into the tree's trunk and then covered over whereas Mr Knights believes that the aerial was on the hut's roof. Memories are often clouded, especially when recalled decades after the event.

Beatrice Temple, who visited all IN-Station sites regularly and diligently took notes of the names of the people she met there and of the issues discussed with them, inexplicably not even once mentions the station at Ousden. Only four of the altogether 20 AU ATS officers who were still employed at closedown came from the West Suffolk Sub-district. A Part II Order (Officers ATS), Serial No 42 - published on 21 July 1944 by authority of WOUM 112/ATS AG 16 (o) *(War Office Unclassified Memorandum, Adjutant General's Branch 16 (officers)* - lists their names as Marina Bloxam (301325), Eleanor N Norman-Butler (205713), JH Chesney (244726) and JP Pratten (248958). This appears to have been the team based at Ousden. They were struck off the strength of Auxiliary Units and posted to No 1 War Office Holding Unit and struck off the Lodging List and Food (allowance) with effect from 25 July 1944.

Norwich IN-Station

Call sign: Bowling

Situated on high ground, possibly the highest ground in the area, the location was obviously carefully chosen. The Forward HQ of the Norfolk Division (later 76th) was based at nearby Sprowston Hall. The first IN-Station hut presumably stood in the extensive grounds of the Hall. When the dugout site was chosen, sometime in 1942, however, there was no need for finding a suitable spot for, or to build a hut, because an ideally suited folly tower already existed. It was soon put to good use.

Frank Hewitt - an AU Signals corporal who, together with a small team was in charge of servicing wireless stations in Hampshire, Lincolnshire and in Scotland, recalls:

> "In 1942, I spent a short time in Norwich, being taught the rudiments of the special (TRD) set by some ATS officers at the top of some tower in the grounds of some big house."

No plausible explanation as to why the chosen site was located in the extensive grounds of a large civilian-owned property, which was not used by the military, has as yet to surface. It is probably due to its private and secluded location that seven decades later the dugout was found in a very good and undisturbed condition. The exit opening was secured with concrete slabs that were covered by a thick layer of soil, and the entrance opening was found still solidly capped with the original reinforced concrete. Because this IN-Station dugout is the best preserved of all such structures known to-date, it merits a detailed description - starting at the exit, which in our case was the point of entry. At the exit end, a concrete culvert pipe emerges into a manhole shaft with breezeblock walls. The top row of breezeblocks appears to have been knocked off in order to lower the shaft for better concealment when the dugout was sealed in 1944. The hatch consisted of wooden or plywood boards, nailed onto two lengths of 2 x 3 inch timber. The hatch would have been attached to two metal pipes - passing through wooden battens for support and then through the boards - and fixed in place by a nut at each side. Each of the pipes was contained within a sleeve made from shorter lengths of (slightly larger diameter) steel pipes were clamped to a wooden frame with two C-brackets. When activated, a counterweight would have descended downwards until it had reached the bottom of a rectangular hole in the floor. Simultaneously, the two long pipes, held within their sleeves, were pushed upwards, resulting in the trapdoor being gradually raised horizontally above ground level *(see page 41)*. Above ground, the trapdoor would have been hidden under a layer of earth.

View into the emergency exit shaft and adjoining escape tunnel

Bundle of sash weights (25 kg) serving as a counterweight for the trapdoor securing the exit opening, found in situ at the bottom of the exit shaft.

There is evidence of the existence of two 240V cables, running parallel to each other along the whole length of the tunnel which suggests that the dugout was connected to mains power. At Norwich, where more original features have survived than at any other of the IN-Stations that have to-date been discovered, some of the fixtures and part of the wiring is still in situ, although wires were cut and switches and sockets removed from panels and switchboards. Norwich is the first IN-Station where two separate electric circuits, one powered by 6V batteries, the other by mains electricity, have been documented (*Simak & Pye*). There is evidence of altogether three switch units, with the wooden panel situated immediately where the exit tunnel enters the dugout. These appear to have been the main point where both external (AC mains) and internal (battery) power were connected into the internal wiring. The main isolating switches for turning off all the power would have been on this panel but no trace remains. The wires were fed through conduits with inspection covers at each bend. The conduit running along the ceiling of the wireless room contained two pairs of ceramic ceiling roses from which, it appears, flexes were leading down to bulb holders with bulbs.

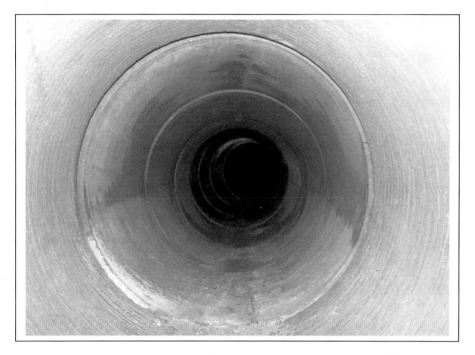

The emergency escape tunnel is 17 metres long. The concrete pipes have an exterior lining of sheet metal, presumably to keep out dampness. This view was taken looking towards the exit opening.

Mains power appears to have come from either a nearby dwelling (house) or from a nearby electricity transformer or substation. The twin conductor cables were used for this purpose. The cables were connected in parallel to halve the resistance thus reducing the voltage drop under load. Mains power would have allowed for decent lighting and fan-assisted ventilation, and possibly also for background heating to keep the dugout dry and remove condensation, and perhaps even for such possible luxuries like a small kettle. Mains could also have been used for trickle-charging the batteries. Further research has since brought to light that the Halstead and Shipley IN-Stations appear to also have been connected to mains power and it is not unreasonable to assume that there were more. In this context, however, it is important to consider the reliability of mains power in wartime. Most mains power was not locally generated and the grid was vulnerable to storm, sabotage or battle damage etc. The wireless sets were designed to run on 6V DC (battery power) and the vulnerability of mains power meant it could never replace batteries and generators.

The exit tunnel emerges into a buried Nissan-type hut consisting of three rooms which are separated thick breezeblock walls. The rooms were accessed through wooden doors that are still in place, functional and in good condition. The room immediately adjoining the escape tunnel was the generator room. Looking back towards the tunnel opening, evidence can be seen that the opening was blocked off where it emerges into the generator room. The cover appears to have been made from wooden boards and some of the screws to fix it to the wall are still in place, embedded in the surrounding breezeblocks. In all likelihood this small room would have been used for housing a battery charging generator, for storing and charging the batteries used for powering the wireless sets as well as the lighting. The whitewashed wall above one of the two small glazed ceramic vent pipes in the breezeblock end wall appears to be soot-stained, indicating that the pipe was probably used for externally ventilating the generator's exhaust fumes. A fire bucket - a sand-filled ration container with an improvised wooden handle - stands by the wall beside the twin doors leading into the wireless room.

It has been documented (*Alf Ellis' diary*) that three sets comprising two batteries each per IN-Station were in regular use. It has also been documented that under training conditions (pre-invasion) batteries were collected by AU Signals maintenance men and taken away for re-charging. In the event of an invasion, IN-Station operators would have had to change and recharge the batteries themselves and for this they required a generator. Two large inlet and outlet ventilation pipes traverse the generator room but most wireless dugouts also had one or two glazed ceramic ventilation pipes, one emerging into the generator room through the wall above the tunnel opening. This pipe appears to have served the purpose of allowing expanded warm air to dissipate, especially when the generator was running and the air in the generator room was heating up.

To charge the batteries, the generator would have to run for about nine hours with its engine getting quite hot. A second, similar ceramic pipe is frequently found near the right-hand corner and not far above floor level. This pipe is believed to have served the purpose of extracting the generator's exhaust fumes by inserting the flexible exhaust pipe into this ceramic pipe. Great care would have been taken to seal it with fireclay or asbestos matting so as to prevent any poisonous carbon monoxide from entering the generator room. The generator would need to have stood on the floor near this pipe, in a position where it would also have been easy to crank-start, refuel and maintain.

Space in the generator room would have been much restricted because batteries, petrol, oil and kerosene in cans and distilled water for topping up batteries would have been stored there, and additional space would have been taken up by a number of fire buckets, required for sprinkling sand over any spilled fuel on the floor, as a fire would have been lethal, not to mention the danger of an explosion. There was a considerable risk of overfilling the generator when refuelling, as there was no gauge.

The process of recharging the batteries took approximately nine hours and was a messy and hazardous task. Cell vents had to be opened before charging so as to avoid electrolyte being forced out of the cells by gassing pressure. During the second phase of charging the accumulators started gassing as excess electrical energy was breaking down the water diluting the acid, into hydrogen and oxygen. This created a dangerous and explosive mixture. The fine mist of acid dispersing with the bubbles was even in those days considered a health hazard. Any electrolyte lost through 'gassing' would have to be topped up with distilled water. The charging of batteries appears to have been controlled from the wireless room. Unpainted areas that remain on the walls after the removal of shelves give some idea as to their size and use. At Norwich *(also Hollingbourne, Shipley and Halstead)*, the outline of the Lyons generator charging switchboard, measuring roughly 60 x 50 centimetres, can still quite clearly be discerned on the wall in the wireless room. Evidence of the special connector cable between the charging switchboard and the Lyons generator, and the gap where up to six individual wires to connect up to the three banks of batteries under charge would have been fed through the wall, supports this. The charging switchboard panel was designed specifically for the use with a Lyons 550W generator, which conveniently answers the question as to what make of generator would have been used at this particular IN-Station.

Suggestions that these generators might have been run while on shelves or benches are without merit because the height of a bench or a shelf would have made cranking difficult and the generator would need to be firmly fixed to it. Of the two types of charging engines used only the Chorehorse had a starter button in addition to a pull cord starter. The Lyons had to be cranked with a starter handle. Refuelling would also have been problematic, considering that Jerry or 4-gallon petrol cans would have been used and that it was tricky even when using a funnel. Furthermore, the generator's weight alone, not to mention its vibrations when running, would have made its positioning anywhere other than on the floor impracticable. Bearing in mind that the primary source of carbon monoxide (CO) is from exhaust fumes and that CO is a colourless, odourless, tasteless and initially non-irritating toxic gas - which makes it very difficult for people to detect - there is no merit in the notion that generators were ever situated in wireless rooms, as indeed no evidence in wireless rooms of the existence of pipes or of openings that could have accommodated generator exhaust pipes has been found. Moreover, the noise and smell would make working very difficult.

As already mentioned, one side the generator room is traversed by two large concrete ventilation pipes, one near the bottom (the inlet pipe) and one near the roof (the outlet pipe). Both of these pipes have a small rectangular opening, which provided ventilation in the generator room. The inlet pipe opening would have been closed – in this case by a homemade collapsible screen constructed from sections of Union Cloth anti-gas (a felt-like fabric impregnated with paraffin oil) nailed to wooden battens – when the generator was running. This may have been to prevent fumes entering the ventilation system of the wireless room.

The wireless room is separated from the generator room by sturdy wooden twin doors with a raised threshold in-between. "DANGER – 250 VOLTS – KEEP OUT" was written in large letters on the inner door with a red crayon, and is still clearly visible – confirming the presence of mains electricity in the generator room. Both doors are covered with a layer of Union cloth - affixed all the way around their outer rims. The doors had to be well sealed so as to protect the operators in the wireless room from the toxic gasses created by the charging of the batteries as well as from the exhaust fumes generated by the charging engine or explosive vapours from petrol cans. Janet Purves-Smith, an ATS officer who worked at Alnwick IN-Station for about 18 months recalls that when the generator was running, the felted doors separating the wireless room from the generator room were always kept shut tight.

> "A charging engine produces an awful lot of carbon monoxide fumes and we had these enormous felted doors which closed through to where the Elsan and the charging engine stood. When you put on the charging engine the doors were completely closed and the vents came into full use and got rid of the exhaust fumes." *(Stephen Sutton, IWM 14817, 18 Nov 1994)*

Despite all precautions, accidents did happen. Cpl Gabbitas recalls that during an exercise (in the Winchester area), which required staying underground for a lengthy period, Sgt Ellis had collapsed and that his unconscious body had to be manhandled up and out of the entrance shaft, accidentally breaking his nose in the process.

Inlet ventilation pipe and cable duct with wiring panel, which also shows wires for connecting the 6 V batteries, next to the escape tunnel opening. On the floor below the panel the Union Cloth screen.

The twin doors separating the generator room from the adjoining wireless room. Note the dark Union Cloth fabric adhering to the doors' edges. This fabric was used to prevent generator exhaust fumes and poisonous gasses from penetrating into the adjoining chamber where the operators worked and slept.

Note the two circular objects seen on the floor below the darker area, where the battery charging board used to be attached to the wall. These blanks or plugs could be used to close the openings of the ventilation pipes when the dugout was not manned to prevent dampness or vermin from entering. They could also allow the wireless room to be sealed off from the outside in the event of an enemy gas attack.

The floor of the wireless room is covered with precisely laid concrete paving slabs which in turn were covered by a layer of brown linoleum, small sections of which are still in place - some bearing the indents of objects that once stood on them. The breezeblock end walls are whitewashed and the corrugated sheeting is painted off-white.

Three aerial feeder cables disappear through the wall at about 40 centimetres above floor level near the entrance doorway. The table for the wireless sets would probably have stood along the wall near this corner in the vicinity of the aerial feeder cables.

The following information comes from Corporal Arthur Gabbitas, who served with Auxiliary Units Signals:

> "The wireless set used was code-named TRD. It was housed in a metal case measuring about 0.40 x 0.24 x 0.23 cm and powered by a large conventional 6-volt 85 AH accumulator battery [sic], the voltage of which was boosted to 240V by a vibrator contained within the set. The frequency used ranged from 48 to 65 mcs, pre-digital commonly used by BBC1 TV. The aerial terminals were connected inside via a piece of flat twin feeder and to a 72-ohm flat twin feeder outside the front panel, leading to the dipole antenna hidden in a tree."

The remains of three aerial feeder cables as they emerge into the wireless room

Above ground, part of one of the aerial feeder cables can still be seen high up on a pine tree.

The lighting in the dugout was provided by two different circuits - one 250 volt AC mains circuit connected to an external source of mains power, and a totally separate circuit for silent, 6V DC battery-powered running of lights, ventilator fans (where provided) and the wireless sets.

Ceramic ceiling roses in the wireless room. One held a battery-powered 6V 6A "Sunshine" light bulb, the adjoining bulb would have been 40 Watt and powered by mains electricity.

The interior (wireless room) side of the entrance door is covered entirely with Union Cloth (anti-gas). The other side of this door, however, appears to be something different entirely. Coming down the entrance shaft, the uninitiated would have found themselves in a small room that to all intents and purposes was used for storage, with a small water tank standing against the wall on one side. On the wall facing the entrance shaft an intruder would have seen a storage shelf, stacked with boxes and tins. This shelf was designed to have the appearance of a bookcase, with a frame extending to both sides of the doorframe (overlapping it) and also to above the door. The wooden brackets that would have supported the removable shelves are still in place and the door itself has small recesses so that the shelves fitted partially into it, perfectly concealing both the door and the doorframe when the shelves were in place and the door closed. The shelf boards are missing but the bookcase-style frame is in situ – and it is the only one known to be still in existence.

179

The section extending to above the door lintel has two lengths of wood affixed to the panels covering the wall. These lengths of wood, one on each side, appear to be fixed in place by two screws, one at each end. Only the top screw, however, holds the piece of wood on the right hand side. The bottom 'screw' is in fact a nail, and a dummy at that. This piece can be moved sideways and in doing so it reveals a small carved out recess and a hole drilled through it. The hole is just large enough to allow for a piece of string to pass through. The other end of this string is still tied to the door catch (on the wireless room side), which could be released by pulling said string, and the wireless room could then be entered by swinging forwards the door - but not without first removing at least some of the shelves. The shelves could then be replaced and the door closed.

Secret door disguised as a storage shelf, leading from the lobby into the wireless room

The antechamber or lobby by the entrance shaft still houses the original 50-gallon water tank, covered with a piece of sheet metal. Beside it there are two fire buckets filled with sand, presumably discarded ration containers, with improvised wooden handles and filled with sand. The walls of the entrance shaft, the breezeblock end wall of the lobby and the corrugated sheeting in this room were not painted. The floor is covered with concrete paving slabs. The room does not contain any other items, but a chemical toilet (Elsan) might once have stood by the wall opposite the water tank. Auxiliers had instructions to use Elsans for the evacuation of faeces only, and that drainpipes or sumps in their OBs were to be used for urination. In cases where drains or sumps were unavailable, tins or bottles with screw caps were to be used.

The drop down entrance-shaft faces the secret doorway into the wireless room. A wooden or steel ladder appears to have been used for access. A large heap of concrete rubble is lying on the floor of the shaft. Presumably this rubble has come from removing the top layers of breezeblocks, in order to hide its presence when the opening was capped after closedown. Running down the wall to the left of the entrance shaft there is a cast iron pipe which ends at about 50 centimetres above floor level. It appears to have been the only source of ventilation in the antechamber.

The 50-gallon water tank, still three quarters full, and two fire buckets stand beside it, in the entrance lobby.

Viewed from below, the entrance opening is now covered with wooden boards. Almost at the top of the breezeblock shaft wall there are several small rectangular recesses. These probably held the wooden frame that surrounded the opening and probably supported the entrance hatch. After removing the hatch and the top layer of breezeblocks, the wooden frame appears to have been pulled off the walls and smashed. Pieces of it, intermingled with lumps of shattered breezeblocks in all sizes, rest in a quite a formidable heap at the bottom of the shaft. Buried amongst it there were a couple of pulleys, and the cast lead counterweights which were used for operating the hatch. When the station was closed down and abandoned in 1944, the top of the shaft was capped with concrete. Once set, this concrete cap was covered by a thick layer of soil. It is still as solid as it was on the day it was capped seven decades ago.

The cast lead counterweights were found buried under the rubble at the bottom of the entrance shaft. As both the size and the quantity of the counterweights would have been defined by the finished weight of the trapdoor, the weights in all likelihood would have been made on site.

All IN-Stations were stripped bare before they were capped at closedown. The following list, compiled from information contained in a contemporary manuscript *(by A Monck-Mason, an ATS wireless operator)*, gives a fairly accurate picture as to what would have been found in an IN-Station dugout at the time it was in use. No differentiation is being made between IN-Station huts and dugouts and the list refers to a handful of the later networks only *(Omagh, Golding, Chirnside, Byfield and Osterley)*, but it may be assumed that it would have applied, with perhaps minor variations, to all existing IN-Stations. The original handwritten list covers two pages and includes items that IN-Stations were supplied with, such as:

> "1 Charging set 550W (Lyons) complete with *(charging)* panel etc, 2 Aerials made up spare complete; 6 Batteries 85 AH; 1 Table barrack folding". Other items found on the list are: "1 TRD Complete Station" and "1 TRD Spare; 1 Lamp electric No1 *(the old bicycle lamp torch)*; electric light wiring, switches, plugs; sockets, lamp holders, shades; Lamp electric 6V 6W *presumably bulbs for the DC lights)* and Lamp electric 230V 40W as well as a field telephone and "1 or 2 Telephones, spare" *(presumably for communications with the "Met" hut).*

Part of a GPO telephone junction box was found in situ on one of the panels in the generator room at Norwich. The telephone wire was not contained within the conduit, which is evidence of good wiring practice. The wireless room is believed to also have contained a number of metal barrack bunk beds. No trace of the latter has been found, suggesting that they may have been metal barrack bunks which would have been returned with everything else before the stations were closed down.

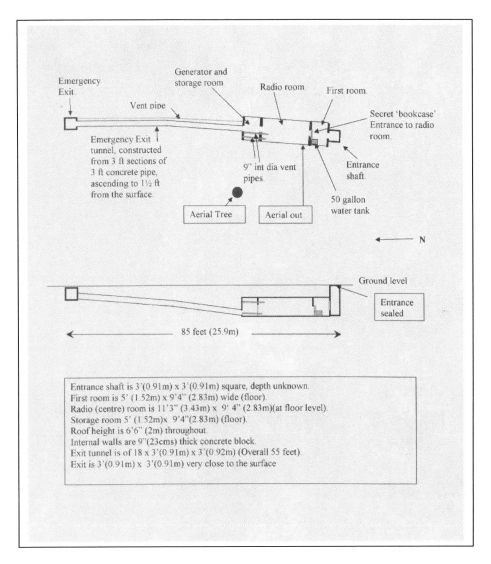

Norwich IN-Station plan drawing

Beatrice Temple is known to have visited the Norwich IN-Station five times, starting in November 1941. In June 1942 she stayed overnight when participating in a night exercise. After having visited the "new site" (presumably the newly constructed dugout) in July 1942, Miss Temple's visits stop. An explanation can be found in an amendment to the May 1942 War Establishment, which suggests that Royal Signals personnel (AU Signals) gradually took over the running of the IN-Stations.

> "In order not to interrupt the working of installations it is requested that surplus ATS and Signals personnel are not returned to their respective corps until a proper handover in each individual case can be carried out." (Memorandum dated April 1942).

Aylsham OUT-Station

The probably best-documented OUT-Station in Norfolk was located in a house called "The Beeches", located on the outskirts of the picturesque market town of Aylsham, near Blickling Hall, in the Broadland district. "The Beeches" was the home of Dr Alec George Holman and his wife Kathleen, who was one of the town's ambulance drivers during the war. Dr Holman is still well known in the historic market town of Aylsham, where he is fondly remembered as a no-nonsense doctor who had little patience for malingerers but was fully committed to his calling - so much so that on one occasion he interrupted a family holiday, driving several hundred miles back to Aylsham, where one of his patients about to give birth had requested his assistance. The road where the family used to live has since been renamed Holman Road in his honour.

The doctor's daughter, Jill, was 16 years old when she was enrolled:

> "Colonel *[sic]* Collings, the local commanding officer *[sic]*, asked my father if he thought I'd fold up at the sight of a German. My father told him I didn't fold up at anything - horses, bulls, and schoolmistresses - so the Colonel *[sic]* recruited me. He thought a brat on a horse was unlikely to be suspected of anything. So I was to ride out and spot any choice targets, in terms of troops or supply dumps."

Jill Monk, nee Holman, in 2012 *(Photo: Katie Hart)*. The Holman's former family home, "The Beeches", in 2012. The house has since been converted into two dwellings. The coal cellar that housed the wireless set is still there but access to it has long since been blocked.

Maj John Collings was a professional soldier and an accomplished equestrian, horse trainer and breeder. Before the war he was a valued member of the Army Polo Team. What Jill did not appear to have known is that Maj Collings was employed by Special Operations Executive and had already spent some time abroad. At the time Jill Holman met Maj Collings he was, unbeknown to her, serving as the Special Duties Branch Intelligence Officer for Norfolk. He was replaced in spring 1944, when Capt Douglas Ingrams RA from Taunton, Somerset, took over. The Major was a frequent guest at the Holman family home, often enjoying a hack on one of Jill's horses.

When duty called him away for longer periods he used to leave his dog, Mark, in Jill's care. Mark was a German shepherd dog, trained to carry ammunition in a special pouch. Once he was injured whilst on a tour of duty on the Continent but rather than leave him to his fate, Maj Collings took the sedated dog, wrapped in a thick blanket, with him all the way to the port of Ostend and from there to England, where Mark received a life-saving blood transfusion at "Millbank" Military Hospital in London. Mark's life was saved at the time but later the dog stood on a landmine and lost a leg and the sight in one eye. He died in 1952 in Germany. His gravestone bears the inscription: "Mark – ein treuer Freund" *(Mark - a faithful friend).*

After initially being kept hidden in the garden shed, the Holmans' wireless set was later installed in the family home's coal cellar, which during the war had been converted to an air raid shelter. It was situated below what at the time was used as the billiard room, and accessed through a hatch in the floor, concealed by a rug. The set was placed in the former coal chute, which had been sealed, and hidden behind an asbestos board with an electric fire fixed to it. By pressing a concealed catch, the board plus the adhering stove could be lifted off. Messages were dropped from the yard above down a pipe leading into the chute. The aerial was disguised as a lightning conductor on the roof.

The Holman family home has long since changed ownership and was converted into two separate dwellings. What used to be the billiard room is now the kitchen in Beeches Dairy. The kitchen has since been fitted with a new tiled floor, effectively blocking access to the cellar beneath.

Aldborough OUT-Station

Dr Eddy's former home and surgery in the village of Aldborough *(picture taken in 2012).*

Just as at Aylsham, where the wireless operator was a doctor, the SUBOUT-Station at Aldborough was also operated by a doctor - Dr James Angwin Eddy. The two doctors had, in fact, known each other for quite some time and until 1933 owned a joint medical practice. The station relayed messages between the Norwich IN-Station and an OUT-Station nearer the coast, further to the north-west.

Dr Eddy worked as a general practitioner in the village from 1923 until 1973. In 1959 he was elected president of the Norwich Medico-Chirurgical Society and for many years, even after his retirement, he served on the Norfolk Local Medical Committee. In his obituary *(October 1995)* it is mentioned that Dr Eddy had many interests, particularly music. What the obituary did not mention is that in the 1940s, Dr Eddy had a wireless set hidden in his surgery that was used to pass on information to the Norfolk IN-Station.

Interestingly, Dr Eddy features in auxilier John Everett's (corporal of Alby Patrol, Norfolk Group 3) memoirs:

> "Although meant to be secret, the location of our OB was certainly known to one or two other people, including Dr Eddy, a local doctor whose job it was to carry written messages to the patrol by placing them into a buried tin can at the foot of a telegraph pole near Hagon Beck bridge (about 50 yards distant from the OB's patrol)."

AU operational patrols and AU Signals worked independently and did not usually know of each other's existence even when operating in the same area. This is one of the rare occasions where it can be shown that they did in fact interact with each other. Although Corporal Everett knew Dr Eddy as a local doctor, and would, in fact, have been registered with him as his local GP, and although he was aware of the doctor carrying messages from and to the dead letterbox of the Alby patrol, he never knew that the doctor's main involvement was in running a secret wireless station for the Special Duties Branch.

Because of her father's acquaintance with Dr Eddy, Jill Monk (nee Holman) too had met the doctor, but like John Everett, whom she also knew, she had - until 2012, when we were able to tell her - never known of both their secret wartime activities. Jill was also unaware that another man she is acquainted with acted as Dr Eddy's courier - the same task that Jill had been carrying out for her father at their OUT-Station in Aylsham. The courier's name is GW "Billy" Hammond and he is still living in the next house up the road from the former doctor's surgery. Mr Hammond recalls that he used to frequently accompany Dr Eddy when he was out in his car, visiting patients. On his own, he would use his bicycle for transport, always carrying with him a tennis racket so that in case he was stopped and questioned, he could explain why he was carrying tennis balls.

Mr Hammond's tennis balls had a small slit cut into them so that a message could be inserted and concealed within, and his job was to take these messages to pre-arranged drop-off points, of which, so he says, they had two. One of these appears to have been the buried tin can remembered by John Everett as having served as his patrol's dead letterbox. At the other the drop-off points Mr Hammond had to wait until he heard the tennis ball hit the bottom; and he always had to use a different route. In his time as a courier or runner, only about four or five messages were ever delivered to each one of the two dead letter boxes, and Mr Hammond recalls that the practice was stopped altogether after about a year.

Southrepps OUT-Station

Southrepps, one of the larger villages along the coast, is situated between the towns of North Walsham and Cromer in the North Norfolk District. The village lies three kilometres inland from the sea and consists of Upper and Lower Southrepps. The wireless set of the Southrepps OUT-Station is believed to have been hidden in the belfry of the parish church of St James. The station was operated by the Vicar, Dr Rev Humphrey Gordon Barclay CVO *(Royal Victorian Order)* MC (1882 – 1955) who lived in the nearby vicarage.

The 15th century tower of St James' church in Southrepps is visible for many miles, and with a height of almost 50 metres it is one of the highest church towers in the county of Norfolk. Height was, of course, paramount to successful wireless communications, which at the time commonly worked by line-of-sight. It has been established that the link to the Norwich IN-Station was line-of-sight.

The Reverend Barclay was born in 1882 in Bletchingley, Surrey, and read Theology at Trinity Hall, Cambridge Theological College. In December 1914 he went to war where - attached to 1st Cavalry Division serving in France - he was a temporary chaplain to the Forces from 1914 – 1919. Earning several campaign medals, including a Military Cross in 1917 "for care and comfort of the wounded under fire" when in action with a front line unit; he did not apply for his medals until 1928. Reverend Barclay is buried near the Barclay family home, Hanworth Hall, and is commemorated in a memorial on the wall of Hanworth St Bartholomew's church.

The British Resistance Organisation Museum at Parham

Colonel JW Stuart Edmondson formally opened the BRO Museum on 30 August 1997, which, to date is the only museum in Britain dedicated to the men and women who served in the various branches of the GHQ Home Forces Auxiliary Units. It is situated on the now disused Parham aerodrome at Silverlace Green, approximately two kilometres to the east of the village of Parham, adjoining the 390th Bombardment Group Memorial Museum housed in the aerodrome's control tower. The museum is sign-posted "Air Museum" from the A12 road to the north of Woodbridge, after passing through Little Glemham.

The Museum is housed in Nissen huts and includes a unique and rare collection of exhibits ranging from Auxiliary Units' weapons and original examples of time pencils and many other paraphernalia with which the men were familiar. The collection also includes uniforms, photographs of patrols and their officers, examples of dead-letter boxes, intelligence instruction dossiers as well as many other Auxiliary Units-related items that have over time been donated by former auxiliers or their families. Pride of place is taken by a reconstructed TRD wireless set. Practical details of the wireless communication networks installed by the Auxiliary Units Signals can also be seen.

A reconstructed operational base - based upon the nearby OB once used by Stratford St Andrew Patrol, which has long since become inaccessible *(see p 120)* - was opened in 2004. Visitors are able to tour this exhibit and hence able to experience for themselves the cramped conditions that the auxiliers had to work in.

If you have skills or interests which you think could help the museum and can spare a few hours a week, please contact them.

390th Bomb Group Memorial Air Museum & The Museum of the British Resistance Organisation

Parham Airfield
Parham
Framlingham
IP13 9AF
Suffolk
England

Phone - 01728 621373

Museum buildings and the former control tower, which houses the 390th Bomb Group Memorial Air Museum

Appendix A

```
                        AUXILIARY UNITS
        ITEMS OUTSTANDING AND STILL REQUIRED FROM PREVIOUS LISTS.


                                              Remarks

1.  HEADQUARTERS, AUXILIARY UNITS

      Knives Fighting              330      HF/3246/Q of 14 Oct 43
                                   125      & HF.1466/G(SD) of
                                            5 Oct 43 refer.  (In
                                            addition to 140 requested
                                            at Appendix 'A')


2.  SPECIAL DUTIES BRANCH, AUXILIARY UNITS.

      Nil.


3.  A.T.S. AUXILIARY UNITS

      Nil.


4.  SIGNALS SECTION, AUXILIARY UNITS

      Batteries Secy, Fort 2v LT     30 )   For Murphy Receivers B81
                                         )  and B93 already supplied:
      Batteries Dry, HT, 120 v       30 )   Authority 6/7/Sigs/2076
                                         )  GR/6/112/F.1
      Microphones Respirators A.G.   16

      Generating Sets, American Onan 2KVA   2

      H.30S Receivers, complete      2

      Charging Sets 300 watt (Chorehorse)   7

      Wireless Receivers (ordinary broadcast  2
                          type)
```

Excerpt from a Stores file. *(The full document, WO 199.936, is held at the National Archives)*

Appendix B

From:- Colonel I.W.R. Douglas.   SECRET

To:- All Members of Special Duties.

You will have heard through your I.O. that the War
Office has decided to "stand down" the Special Duties
organization.

On instructions from the Commander-in-Chief I am en-
closing a copy of his letter to me. In this letter paying
tribute to your splendid services he gives the reasons for
the War Office decision.

The War is undoubtedly going well on all fronts - not
least perhaps in Normandy where our successes, although
not so apparently spectacular as in some other theatres, are
nevertheless very real. However in this respect it is well
to remember that destruction of the enemy forces, rather
than [...] of battle; once the former has been achieved, the latter
follows automatically.

That we are now on the eve of, and fully prepared for,
the greatest tank battle of the War gives some indication
that we have not been slow to take full advantage of the
100% tactical surprise achieved in our landings.

If the outcome of this battle is successful - and we
have cause for reasoned confidence - it will have a far-
reaching influence on the whole future of operations in
the West, if indeed it is not the decisive battle of the
whole campaign.

To find the manpower to maintain the pressure and follow
up our successes, thus tipping the scales definitely in our
favour, will strain to the utmost our already over-taxed
resources, hence the necessity for making available the
handpicked and highly trained regular specialist personnel
of Special Duties.

Now that we have come to the parting of the ways, I must
tell you how proud we all are to have been associated with
this unique organization and for which, latterly, I personally
have had the additional privilege of being responsible.

On behalf of all my officers and myself I would also
like to tell you how much we have admired your disinterested
loyalty which has made constant demands on your time, energy
and initiative, all of which you have so generously and
selflessly given.

Finally for your keenness and enthusiasm which has been
an inspiration to us one and all Thank you.

7 JUL 44   Colonel,
                                                       Commander,
                                                   Auxiliary Units.

Stand-down letter to Special Duties Branch, dated 7 July 1944

191

Appendix C

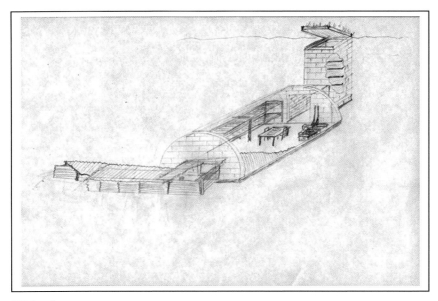

OB drawing

Appendix D

Earlham Home Guard unit with Capt Percy Ernest Turner at centre front row
(Photo source: Mary May nee Turner, in BROM Archive)

192

Appendix E

Event 3. Miniature Rifle Practice - Grouping

        Each man will fire 10 rounds at about 20 yards. One
wide will be allowed.

        A half-inch group wins 5 points; a two-inch group 1 point.

Event 5. **Explosives**

        Any five of ten possible problems will be chosen
each time. In addition a sixth will be set on the spot
which will be allotted to the Patrol Leader.

        Patrols will be marked on the way in which charges are made
up and placed on various targets. They will have to draw
the amount of stores they require from the dump and will lose
marks if they draw too much or too little.

        All priming will be done with CE primers.

        Dummy detonators will be used and safety pins left in all
mechanisms provided with them.

        Each problem will be marked as follows:

            Drawing of stores   5 marks
          Making up charges   10 ..
          Placing of charges   5 ..
          Camouflage   5 ..
          Amount of explosive used 5 ..

Problems

    1. Destroy a dump of land mines in their crates. (Place
       one 1 lb unit charge against the base or side of any
       one mine - not against the pressure plate)

    2. Destroy a dump of separate shells and propellants.
       (Two 1-lb unit charges placed against the side of
       one shell in the dump and two fire-pots initiated
       by time-pencil or 'L' delays placed among the
       propellants)

       To destroy a dump of quick-firing shells place
     two unit charges against the side of one shell in the
    dump.

    3. Destroy a dump of aeroplane bombs.(Place two unit
       charges against the side of a bomb opposite the primer
       hole.

4. Destroy a dump of petrol in cans (Make a combination charge of any incendiary fired with time pencils or 'L' delays, and connected by Orange line to a charge of one CE primer or 2 oz of other explosive fired by a detonator. (as for last year's competition)

5. Destroy a food dump. Fix up a ring of A.W. bottles connected by detonating fuse initiated by two time pencils or 'L' delays and detonators. Only combustible food will be attacked. Detonating fuse to be strapped to side of A.W. bottle, NOT round it.

6. Destroy an aeroplane; two charges to be placed to fire simultaneously. (Place charges so as to destroy either the tail or wings by a blast effect from a charge put in such a position that the blast will penetrate under the skin, and to destroy some mechanical part of the plane by another charge. Connect 2 charges together by detonating fuse fired either by two time-pencils or 'L' delays and detonators.)

7. Destroy a 'B' vehicle, with two simultaneous charges.
   (Place one charge to destroy the engine or gear box and one to destroy the frame or road wheels or both. Connect as in No. 6.)

8. Destroy a gun with two charges. (Set one charge to separate the barrel from the recoil mechanism or to destroy the recoil mechanism; set another to destroy the sights. Connect and fire as in No 6.)

9. Destroy an 'A' vehicle. (Set two unit charges together to remove driving sprocket or wheel or to destroy both the driving sprocket and the track.)

10. Fell a tree in a given direction. See calendar.

11. Set a booby trap to fire a shrapnel mine. See calendar.

12. This will not be announced until the competition.

Take to Syderstone   Denims; food for the day; sniper's veils;
                      rubber boots; revolvers; brassards; safety-match
                      razor-blades or small pocket-knives for cutting
                      fuses.

Wear serge uniforms with all brass polished; leather boots, belts,
      and anklets.

Instructions, Patrol Competition – Document issued by Lt AGD Greenshields, GCO Norfolk Group 4 *(Source: Lt LS Harris, private papers)*

Appendix F

Attack on   Scottow Aerodrome.   8½hrs.

~~Objective~~   Dumps   of   Bombs.

1. Enemy in complete possession. Planes ~~landing~~ → running a shuttle service from Holland. Fighters also arriving + not going back. Dumps along east perimeter. ~~Any~~ ~~~~ ~~British Magazine~~ exploded.

2. To sabotage Bomb dumps. (If circumstances favourable we can try to blow off tails of 2 or 3 planes but this is all secondy)

3. At Dark.

   From O.B.   by   Col... ...? Farm   to   North Farm.
   (Grove House)   ~~Orchard~~ Frank Place's Orchard.
                    6 rows north   6 rows east.

                    Pairs   ~~Nip~~ ~~permits~~ here
   Bill Self left?   Jim? sends.
                              Bert + John next;
   Victor + Jim deft rear.   Arnold + George @ base

4.   Self + Bill to go in thro' wire + attack
Dump B.   + sentries;   Bert + John take up watchy posit.
       Jim + Victor to take Dump A.

Notes in Sgt Harris' handwriting, concerning a planned exercise in form of an attack on Scottow Aerodrome (better known as Coltishall aerodrome) by the men of Hoveton patrol. *(Lt LS Harris, private papers)*

Appendix G

EXPLANATION OF FIG. 112

No.	Name of Artery	Size	Depth below Surface in inches	Loss of Consciousness in seconds	Death
1....	Brachial	Medium	½	14	1½ Min.
2....	Radial	Small	¼	30	2 "
3....	Carotid	Large	1½	5	12 Sec.
4....	Subclavian	Large	2½	2	3½ "
5....	(Heart)	—	3½	Instantaneous	3 "
6....	(Stomach)	—	5	Depending on depth of cut	

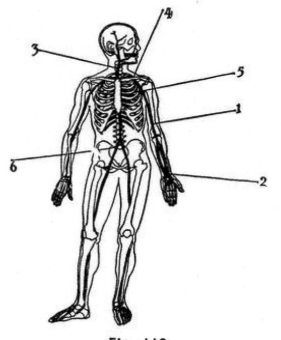

Fig. 112

Excerpt from **"All-in Fighting"** by William E. Fairbairn (1942):
Certain arteries are more vulnerable to attack than others, because of their being nearer the surface of the skin, or not being protected by clothing or equipment. Don't bother about their names so long as you can remember where they are situated. In the accompanying diagram (Fig. 112), the approximate positions of the arteries are given. They vary in size from the thickness of one's thumb to that of an ordinary pencil. Naturally, the speed at which loss of consciousness or death takes place will depend upon the size of the artery cut.

Appendix H

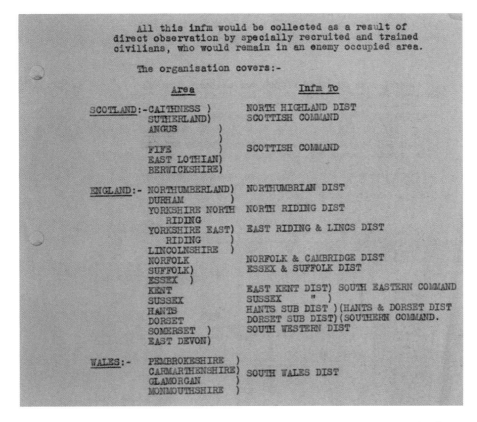

```
        All this infm would be collected as a result of
     direct observation by specially recruited and trained
     civilians, who would remain in an enemy occupied area.

              The organisation covers:-

              Area                      Infm To

   SCOTLAND:-CAITHNESS  )        NORTH HIGHLAND DIST
            SUTHERLAND)          SCOTTISH COMMAND
            ANGUS       )

            FIFE        )        SCOTTISH COMMAND
            EAST LOTHIAN)
            BERWICKSHIRE)

   ENGLAND:- NORTHUMBERLAND)     NORTHUMBRIAN DIST
            DURHAM        )
            YORKSHIRE NORTH       NORTH RIDING DIST
              RIDING
            YORKSHIRE EAST)       EAST RIDING & LINCS DIST
              RIDING      )
            LINCOLNSHIRE  )
            NORFOLK               NORFOLK & CAMBRIDGE DIST
            SUFFOLK)              ESSEX & SUFFOLK DIST
            ESSEX  )
            KENT                  EAST KENT DIST) SOUTH EASTERN COMMAND
            SUSSEX                SUSSEX     "   )
            HANTS                 HANTS SUB DIST )(HANTS & DORSET DIST
            DORSET                DORSET SUB DIST)(SOUTHERN COMMAND.
            SOMERSET   )          SOUTH WESTERN DIST
            EAST DEVON)

   WALES:-  PEMBROKESHIRE   )
            CARMARTHENSHIRE)      SOUTH WALES DIST
            GLAMORGAN       )
            MONMOUTHSHIRE   )
```

Excerpt of file WO 199/1194 *(National Archives)*, detailing where information gathered at the various IN-Stations would have been sent in 1944 *(see also p 162, The local wireless network)*. Army command structure was significantly re-organised twice between 1940 and 1944.

In Eastern Command (which covered both Norfolk and Suffolk), together with Northern Command, South-Eastern Command and Wales (Western Command), all IN-Stations passed their information to their District HQs.

In South-Eastern Command (East Kent District and Sussex District), the Command HQs was also a recipient. Dorset and Hampshire appear to have been special cases as information was passed to Dorset Sub-District HQ or Hampshire Sub-District HQ respectively, plus Hampshire and Dorset District and also Southern Command.

In Scotland, in all but one county the IN-Station passes information to Scottish Command. Caithness reported to Highland District.

Appendix I

570 2/13   IHA

Tel.No.HIGHWORTH 85 Ext20

→ CSO

Subject:- Closing Down - Progress Report.

To: Chief Signal Officer,
Home Forces.

        The following details are submitted for your
information.

IN AND OUT STATIONS (all Areas)

        All Stations dismantled and closed down.   All
dugouts have been blocked as ordered by HQ Auxiliary Units.

        All huts have been cleared and handed over to
local Q.Cs. and G.Es.

        Special Duties Branch, HQ Auxiliary Units have
been advised of clearance and de-requisitioning of land
is now in progress.

STORES

        All Area ledgers have been checked to consolidated
ledgers and have been closed.

WIRELESS SETS

        No.17 Sets and No.36 Sets have been returned to
Woolwich.

        All special sets have been handed over to No.1
S.C.U. Whaddon.

        All batteries 2v 16AH, 6v 16AH and 6v 85 AH
have been disposed of either to C.S.Os. of the various commands or
to Woolwich.

TEST EQUIPMENT.

        These Stores have been returned either to
Woolwich or to No.1 S.C.U.

TOOLS AND COMPONENTS

        These are being returned to Woolwich if ordnance
issue and to No.1 S.C.U if purchased from S.D. funds.

TRANSPORT

        All vehicles from Areas have been concentrated
at this Headquarters and will be retained here for approximately
ten days.   All tools have been checked and completed and the
vehicles have had a workshops inspection.   Drivers are
working on faults found and they will have completed this by
the end of the month.

DOCUMENTS

        All documents in respect of personnel have been
checked and accounted for.

        All documents of a security nature have been checked
and orders for disposal are awaited from H.Q. Aux.Units.

                                  ..../2

Auxiliary Units Signals closedown progress report *(The National Archives)*

Index of Patrols – Norfolk

Index of Patrols - Suffolk

<u>**B.A.3.A.P Cable**</u> - Synopsis of correspondence

The BA 3 AP cable was used by AU Signals as aerial feeder cable. On 24th Aug 1942 the Telegraph Construction & Maintenance Company Ltd acknowledges the receipt of an order No AUX/SD/285 from Major R Signals (address c/o GPO Highworth) for 10,000 yards of said cable. This order was returned with the explanation that it had to be forwarded to the Cable Planning Officer at the Ministry of Supply so that the required raw materials could be allocated. Lt FD Oakey (for Major R Signals) duly forwarded the order on 25th August and a telegram was sent on the 26th. Not having heard back by 16th September, he requested *"May this office now be informed of the position, as this cable is most urgently required"*. Finally, on 28th Sept 1942 the assistant director of the Ministry of Supply/E.S.2.L. wrote to Aux Units Signals:

> "I have instructed the Telegraph Construction and Maintenance Co., to supply the cable required. I should like to remind you that before any cables of this nature are again ordered they must first be referred to this Department."

On 3rd May 1943 another cable order was sent by RMA Jones, Major R Signals, this time to the Cable Planning Officer at the Ministry of Supply:

> "May necessary allocation of raw materials for 10,000 yards of type B.A.3.A.P cable be supplied to Messrs Telegraph Construction & Maintenance Co. Ltd, Telcon Works, Greenwich, please. The cable is required for use of this unit."

Receipt of this order came promptly on 7th May but the assistant director, FH Houghton, was not sure whether the request referred to an order which had already been placed or to a new order. Furthermore, he wrote,

> "We point out that B.A.3.A.P. is a non-standard type and from a production point of view it would be preferable for you to use Duradio 30. You might like to contact Telegraph Construction and Maintenance Co and finalise your requirements before taking further action".

Following this correspondence, Major Jones made further inquiries and confirmed that the cable Duradio 30 was not a suitable replacement for B.A.3.A.P. cable for AU Signals purposes and he repeated his order of 10,000 yards of B.A.3.A.P. cable. The order was received on 12th August 1943. Yet another order for 10,000 yards of cable was placed on 26th April 1944 and another problem was encountered. A letter dated 27th May 1944, the Quartermaster of "Q" Branch of GHQ Home Forces informs that the order had been forwarded to this headquarters by the War Office and he requested an explanation as to why application was made direct to the Ministry of Supply and not through the normal channels and:

> "If it is desired that the matter of release of raw materials be taken up by this Headquarters with War office full particulars of the requirement for the cable should be given".

This time the Commander of Auxiliary Units, Colonel FW Douglas, replied himself:

> "A special grant is available for certain Stores for use in connection with operational wireless nets. It has been the practise in the past to purchase cable from the Telegraph Construction and Maintenance Co. Ltd. Until Sept 1942, orders were passed direct to the firm concerned and supply was made in due course; bills for the cable were paid from the special fund mentioned above. All orders previous to Sept 42 were met without difficulty, but after that date the supplier informed this Headquarters that it would be necessary for the cable Planning Officer to authorise the issue of the raw material."

Select Bibliography:

Field Marshal Lord Alanbrooke, War Diaries 1939-1945 (Phoenix 2002)
Stewart Angell: The Secret Sussex Resistance (Middleton Press 1996)
Michael Calvert: Fighting Mad: One Man's Guerrilla War (2nd ed Leo Cooper Ltd 2004)
Book of Capel: ed. R Pearce (published by Capel Parish Council, 1995)
Albert E Cocks: Churchill's Secret Army 1939-45 (The Book Guild Ltd, Lewes, Sussex 1992)
Andrew Croft: A Talent for Adventure (The S.A.P. Ltd, 1991)
Geoff Dewing: Suffolk's Secret Army 1996
Peter Fleming: Invasion 1940 (Panther Books Ltd 1959)
Adrian Hoare: Standing up to Hitler (Countryside Books 1997, 2002)
Robert Jarvis: Fortress Lowestoft (The Heritage Workshop Centre, Lowestoft 2002)
David Lampe: The Last Ditch (Cassell and Co, 1968)
Simon Paul MacKenzie, The Home Guard (Oxford University Press, 1996)
Paul McCue: SAS Operation Bulbasket (Pen & Sword Military 2007)
Mike Osborne: 20th Century Defences in Britain – Suffolk (Concrete Publications 2006)
Mike Osborne: 20th Century Defences in Britain – Norfolk (Concrete Publications 2008)
Major N.V.Oxenden M.C.: Auxiliary Units History and Achievement 1940-1944
(Reproduction of an original document published by Parham Air Museum)
Mark Sansom: The Secret Army – Wartime Underground Resistance in Lincolnshire
(Heritage Lincolnshire 2004)
Alan Ward: Resisting the Nazi Invader (Constable 1997)
John W Warwicker: Churchill's Underground Army (Frontline Books 2008)
John W Warwicker: With Britain in Mortal Danger (Cerberus Publishing Ltd. 2002)
Alan Williamson: East Ridings Secret Resistance (Middleton Press 2004)

Recommended Websites:

The British Resistance Archive B.R.A. (CART) - www.coleshillhouse.com
Subterrania Britannica – www.subbrit.org.uk
Auxunit News – www.auxunit.org.uk

Civil Defence and Home Guard in Suffolk:
http://civildefence-suffolk.webeden.co.uk/#/auxiliary-units/4546928318